being a girl

Kim Cattrall
and Amy Briamonte

Illustrations by Marf

LITTLE, BROWN AND COMPANY
New York ❧ Boston

Little, Brown and Company

Hachette Book Group USA
1271 Avenue of the Americas, New York, NY 10020
Visit our Web site at www.lb-teens.com

First Edition: October 2006

Library of Congress Cataloging-in-Publication Data

Cattrall, Kim.

    Being a girl / Kim Cattrall — 1st ed.

      p. cm.

ISBN-13: 978-0-316-01102-0 (hardcover)
ISBN-10: 0-316-01102-9 (hardcover)

     1. Cattrall, Kim—Juvenile literature. 2. Teenage girls—Juvenile literature.
     3. Self-esteem in adolescence—Juvenile literature. 4. Adolescent psychology—Juvenile literature. I. Title.

HQ798.C28 2006

158.10835'2—dc22

2005035617

Published by arrangement with
MADISON PRESS BOOKS
1000 Yonge Street, Suite 200
Toronto, Ontario
M4W 2K2 Canada
www.madisonpressbooks.com

10 9 8 7 6 5 4 3 2 1

Printed in Singapore

Contents

A Note from Kim

This year marks my fiftieth birthday and, like most landmarks in life, it's made me take stock of where I've been, where I am, and where I'm going. My life so far has been a lot of fun and hard work. I've taken risks that have paid off and made mistakes that I couldn't change. But I have been lucky enough, and stubborn enough, to stick to what I love to do and have surrounded myself with people who were always there with love and support.

Luck had something to do with these rewards, but so did I. And that's where the idea for this book, *Being a Girl*, came from. I wanted to share with you my personal journey through some of the same challenges and decisions that you're about to face as your world starts to change and expand—so you can be more aware of what's going on around you *and* inside you, and navigate with a little more skill.

One of the things I like most about Samantha Jones, the character I played on *Sex and the City*, is her strong sense of self. She has amazing inner resources to deal with all kinds of situations. Samantha was a wonderful role to play and, because of it, I've had the opportunity to meet and speak with thousands of young women across the country and around the world. And since Samantha is the character on the show who seems to know *everything*, teens of all ages ask my advice—about dating, shopping, losing weight, makeup, friendship, what's hot, what's not. All kinds of questions—from all kinds of girls.

Most of us aren't Samantha Jones—including me. What she has learned and knows is a lot different from what you or I know, and that has to do with individual experience. But it also has to do with asking questions—and knowing what to do with the answers. As Samantha, I've been lucky to have you come to me with your questions. As Kim, I'd like to help you find the answers.

Kim Cattrall
New York City, 2006

Chapter One

BEING A *girl*

As a teenager, I remember feeling that the world seemed designed to keep me in my place. The media, and even most adults, didn't seem particularly interested in young people or in what we had to say. But learning that I could rely on myself made dealing with everything else easier. I imagine growing up today might be even more complicated. Now that the media *are* focusing on youth and teenagers, they do it with laser-like intensity. But while marketers chase the fountain of youth, I'd like to concentrate on another resource—one you should never lose sight of. It's not anything you can find in a perfume bottle, a Gap ad, or even a Manolo Blahnik shoe. In fact, it's not available in stores at all. It's called *self-esteem*, and it comes from within you.

Self-esteem is more than just feeling good about yourself. It's the glue that holds you together when things get uncomfortable or tough. It's a way for you to learn from your mistakes and to trust your gut when it's time to make a decision. Building self-esteem is a process that is never really finished. The key word is "self." It's got to come from you. When I think about what has kept me going, two thoughts come to mind: BELIEVE IN YOURSELF and YOU ARE NOT ALONE.

ME AT 14, THE YEAR I ACTED WITH THE COURTENAY SUMMER THEATER ON VANCOUVER ISLAND.

SELF-ESTEEM

When you have true, well-developed you have a stronger idea not only about yourself but also about the world around you and the culture you live in. The next time you feel you're not beautiful enough, look carefully to make sure someone isn't trying to sell you something or control how you feel about yourself.

Inside OUT

Where does self-esteem come from? On the surface, at least, it can seem to depend on where you live—and when. Every generation of young women wrestles with the demands, fads, and obsessions of the day. Right now, it's been said, "our self-esteem shrinks and grows in front of the mirror." But before fashion shoots, television, and mass marketing, girls were more likely to micro-manage their insides than their outsides.

Check out this page from a girl's diary, written in 1892:

Resolved not to talk about myself or my feelings. To think before speaking. To work seriously. To be self-restrained in conversation and actions. Not to let my thoughts wander. To be dignified. Interest myself more in others.

Self-improvement in 1892 seems to have been all about how you behaved. Modern self-improvement, on the other hand, focuses heavily on dieting and how we look. Have the goals of girlhood changed so radically? Are we more shallow now than girls were back then? The truth is that girls today respond to the pressures around them just as girls always have. What our "consumer culture" asks most clearly of girls today is to buy things and to look good and *thin* in them. Kind of a nutty message to get at a time in your life when you have limited earning potential and your body is changing. But that nineteenth-century diary entry is suffocating in its own way, too. At that time, self-expression and emotional openness were not valued in young women. The willingness of this young girl to give them up is no less sad than our current obsession with looking good.

> The truth is that girls today respond to the pressures around them just as girls always have.

MY 12TH BIRTHDAY, LIVERPOOL, ENGLAND. (COULDN'T WAIT TO GROW UP.)

11

Through Thick and Thin: A Commitment to *yourself*

"No one can make you feel inferior without your consent."

—Eleanor Roosevelt, my favorite First Lady

What I Know NOW

Without a doubt, I was most at odds with my body during my teens. My self-image was put to a rather difficult test during that time. My first professional job as an actress was in a major Hollywood movie with a very famous director. I was seventeen. The film was shot in the south of France around the time of the Cannes Film Festival—an event filled with glitz and glamour. Young, alluring, scantily clad starlets appeared in every hotel lobby and on every beachfront. The cast of our movie included five young actresses, and we were all introduced at a festival press conference as the director's "new stars." I felt every bit a star in a lovely flowered blouse and pink skirt I had bought at Bonwitt Teller, one of my favorite stores in New York City at the time.

After the press conference, the director told me that I had to lose weight—that I was fat. I was 5' 6" and had never weighed more than 115 pounds soaking wet. At first, I thought he was joking. I had been chubby as a young girl and always had a healthy appetite—still do—but was never thought of as being overweight or heavy. I panicked. Suddenly, I was no longer the "Star of Tomorrow" that I had been ten minutes earlier. Now I was fat—and therefore not good enough.

Like a lot of people, I've had long periods when my self-esteem was anything *but* positive. Growing up, I wanted to be smart enough not to have to study and cool enough not to care. Physically, I wanted smaller feet, thinner legs, and—most importantly of all—bigger breasts. My older sister had far bigger ones than my "just a handful." Getting older, I've discovered that "just a handful" is "just enough." (Still not thrilled with the size nine shoe, but what are you going to do?)

What I know now is that caring for and being good to oneself is more important than any idea of being perfect.

13

This experience marked the beginning of **A WEIGHT BATTLE IN MY HEAD** that would stay with me through the rest of my teens and early twenties.

MINUTES AFTER THIS NEWSPAPER PHOTO AT THE CANNES FILM FESTIVAL PRESS CONFERENCE WAS TAKEN, MY SELF-ESTEEM SUFFERED A TREMENDOUS BLOW. (THAT'S ME, THIRD FROM THE RIGHT.)

Back at the hotel, I had a good cry and confided to one of my co-stars about what had happened. She told me that the camera adds at least ten pounds to *anyone* on film—not just *me*. Phew!

I knew that I hadn't gained weight since I'd met the director a month earlier at my audition; I even did my old tried-and-true "blue jeans test" (see page 16), just to be sure. This made me feel much better, but I still had to lose the weight.

I asked her for suggestions. She rattled off a list of fad diets, like eating only apples and yogurt for weeks. I had also heard of other girls sticking their fingers down their throat or starving themselves. Definitely not for me. There didn't seem any way that I was going to lose ten pounds in the four days left before shooting started. It was heartbreaking to think that on my first professional job I wasn't perfect.

I knew I wasn't overweight, but just to be on the safe side, I cut back on desserts and bread and ran on the beach in the mornings. I felt I was doing everything I could, and that was all that should be asked of me. Still, I had to endure criticism and badgering from this bully—who was overweight himself.

This experience marked the beginning of a weight battle in my head that would stay with me through the rest of my teens and early twenties. I was now living with the devastating idea that I was too fat to be employed as an actress.

Looking back, I wish I'd been able to block out the director's cruelty. I know now that what he was raging about had nothing to do with me, really. He was a miserable man who couldn't recognize who he had hired—a seventeen-year-old talented, vulnerable, chubby-cheeked girl.

A few years later, I was under contract at Universal Studios, and the weight issue came up again. But this time, I was more prepared. I found a good nutritionist and began to understand my body type and what I needed to do to stay slim *and* healthy.

I followed my doctor's advice and learned to work with my appetite. I also learned that exercising regularly is key to looking great and being healthy. The earlier you set up this routine for yourself, the easier it'll be to make it part of your everyday life.

I still watch what I eat daily and exercise at least three times a week. My workout has changed over the years, but for my body type I always include a strong cardio session.

THE BLUE JEANS TEST

At 5' 7", my ideal weight is between 132 and 135 pounds. That's more than models weigh, but it's how I feel and look my best. It's also a weight I know I can comfortably maintain while still eating well (which I love to do) and exercising. But I don't weigh myself too often. I've found that scales make me too obsessive. Instead, I own a pair of blue jeans that fit great and are most comfortable when my weight is just right. When I'm feeling heavy, or I've been overindulging, I try on those jeans. If they're tight, or—worst-case scenario—I have to lie down on my back to get the zipper up, I know it's time to cut back on the desserts and bread and step up the cardio!

Learning to look after yourself is part of a well-rounded education that you will benefit from your whole life. But you can't do it alone or by skimming an article in a fashion mag. Without the support of a doctor, my family and friends, and a nutrition and exercise regimen that worked for me, I'd still be out there looking for the easy answers and turning myself —and my body—inside out. Today's emphasis on body image can't be denied. And it can't be totally ignored. The trick is to keep it in perspective and take from it the good things that can make *you* healthier and more creative. Sure, Samantha was seductive, but it was her confidence and charm that really drew people to her. How else could she have gotten through those many bad-hair/ strange-outfit days?

Remember, no matter what other people think about you—fat or skinny, smart or cool— it's how you feel about yourself that matters.

AS SAMANTHA, TAKING CARE OF BUSINESS.

17

WHAT ARE BIG GIRLS MADE OF?

How to develop self-esteem is not a secret, it's a skill—one that we learn throughout the course of our lives. Here's my recipe.

Ingredients:
- **CONNECTION** (relationships with other people)
- **MASTERY** (being capable)
- **ASSERTIVENESS** (standing up for what you believe in)
- **FLEXIBILITY** (the ability to adapt and consider new ideas or routines)
- **SELF-CONTROL** (the ability to control your own impulses)
- **COMPASSION** (empathy and kindness)

If you're like me, working on this could keep you busy for a long while, so don't expect to get there overnight. There are lots of times when we all have to...well, improvise.

Fake It Till You Make It

New challenges and situations can be scary. Maybe a minute ago you were feeling fine. Now, getting up in front of the class, trying out for a team or band, or even just walking into a room full of people you'd like to know better, your heart pounds, cheeks flush, and knees wobble. In your mind you're thinking, "What's going on, and how can I make it stop?!"

The feeling can be so unsettling it might keep you from putting yourself in new situations. But if you keep avoiding challenges, you will never learn to master them, which will eventually lessen your self-esteem. You need to take matters in hand. (Check out **Six Ways to Keep Your Cool**, next page.)

Being afraid does not mean that you aren't courageous.

It's been said that bravery is acting in the presence of fear. After all, if you aren't afraid, there's no need for bravery.

"Everyone thought I was
bold and fearless and
even arrogant, but inside
I was always quaking."

—Katharine Hepburn

19

Six Ways to Keep Your *COOL*

1. **TRY NOT TO OVERREACT TO FEAR**

It's normal to feel fear when the stakes are high, and for your body to react with a racing pulse and dry mouth. These signals are meant to alert you that something you care about is at risk. The symptoms of fear are really not so terrible; we experience similar sensations when we're really happy. You are *not* dying and you *are* capable of overcoming these physical sensations.

2. **DON'T** BEAT YOURSELF UP

Even after years of acting, I can still get nervous before going on stage or in front of the camera, but I no longer think of this negatively. In fact, it's when I *don't* feel a little something in my stomach that I know what I'm doing hasn't got my juices flowing yet. I think of nerves as my talent talking to me. It's telling me that I care and want to do well, and that I'm excited and invested in what I'm doing.

3. **RESIST** NEGATIVE THOUGHTS

When the symptoms of fear well up inside, don't think negatively. Instead, say to yourself, "I'm ready. I feel good. I feel focused. I feel powerful. This is how people feel when they're about to kick butt!"

4. **CALM** YOURSELF

For me, the quickest way to calm down is simply to make a conscious effort to breathe, deeply. I find a quiet spot and take five slow, deep breaths. I breathe in through my nose for five counts, hold for five, and exhale for five. Try this before a test, a job interview, or even before going on a date.

5. RELAX YOUR MUSCLES

Experts have shown that muscle tension always goes along with anxiety. It's what we mean when we say "uptight." Nervousness and anxiety are actually supported and reinforced by tense muscles. Try to notice the muscle groups that tense up when you're under pressure, and then practice relaxing them one by one. Relaxing your muscles sends a positive message through your body that you are not under threat—and that makes it much easier to stay calm.

6. CONFRONT YOUR FEARS

Coping with fear improves with practice. So instead of avoiding situations that may frighten you, try to see them as an opportunity to develop coping skills. You will learn to put less emphasis on the outcome of each situation and more on the process of building confidence. Then, when a *truly* terrifying situation comes along, you will be that much more ready to handle it.

Whether you learn to conquer fear or embrace it, there's at least one more thing you'll need to master along the way. (On the next page, you'll see what I mean.)

Oops!
I Did it Again

When you're younger, it seems like the world is filled with accomplished people who have limitless confidence and endless supplies of self-esteem. I've learned, that is *not* the whole story. Behind every achievement—whether it's an Olympic gold medal, a weekly paycheck, or a well-cooked meal—lies a story rich in mistakes, experimentation, and failure. We all make mistakes. The point is to learn as much as you can from them. A director I once worked with told me he waits for mistakes to happen on set because they force actors to react honestly in the moment instead of by rote. In short, sometimes what we consider a failure can be more instructive than success.

If you have never failed, it might mean that you've never tried anything new, never attempted to push past your limits, or challenged yourself. If you think of failure as the end, then you've really lost. If you think of failure as a beginning, you're that much closer to your next success—even if it means making a few different choices along the way.

"It's better to explore life and make mistakes than to play it safe. Mistakes are all part of the dues one pays for a full life."

—Sophia Loren

Mixed Messages

We can't always control what goes on around us, but one thing we can take charge of is the way we treat ourselves. There is only one way to do it—with respect.

Like many people, I never needed much help in finding things wrong with myself, because I've always been my own harshest critic. Growing up, I was upset over not just what I saw in the mirror but also what I felt inside. Doing badly on a chemistry exam or being called clueless because I didn't recognize a popular Rolling Stones tune could turn my stomach to lead.

When you're down, don't make things worse by kicking yourself. You wouldn't say "You're so fat" or "You're such a loser" to a friend, so why would you talk to yourself this way? You may feel that you're only trying to be honest with yourself—but self-awareness and self-abuse are two different things. The first is good; the second is dangerous. Want to know how you can lighten up without letting yourself off the hook? Watch your language.

Try this test: in the course of a day, *every time* you have a negative thought about yourself, no matter how silly, write it down. At the end of the day, read back the list, and see how you talk to yourself—it's an eye-opener.

So, how do you stop beating yourself up? First, don't send yourself hateful, hopeless messages. Then, take a look at the problem you need to keep sight of and rephrase it in a positive way. Instead of thinking "I'm so fat," think "I'd like to lose weight." "Boys don't like me" becomes "I haven't connected with a boy yet." Change "I can't find a job" to "I'm looking for a job." You can't always control the way the world treats you, but you *can* control the way you treat yourself.

"The bird sings not because it has an answer. The bird sings for it has a song."

—Poet Maya Angelou

Talking to *yourself*

Many young women dream of telling the world who they are, just as I did—but first, we have to tell ourselves. You might think, "Why should I write down my own thoughts when I already know what they are?" But writing things down can help you discover a great deal—not only what you are looking for but also how you're thinking and feeling. We struggle with the BIG ideas (Who am I? What am I going to do with my life? What do I believe in?) and the more mundane (Does this look good on me? Am I popular? Will he call?). These are all basic questions that will never go away entirely.

The next time you're sitting around waiting for practice/rehearsal/detention to start, write down some things about yourself, just to see how they fit:

- **Stuff you're good at;** *stuff you're not.*
- **Things you like about yourself;** *things you don't.*
- **What makes you feel fantastic;** *what doesn't.*
- **Some of your goals;** *some of your worries.*

Read the lists carefully. If what you've written doesn't feel right, maybe you're not being honest with yourself. Start again.

ME AT 15, REHEARSING PUCK IN THE PARK. I'M SMILING BECAUSE I JUST GOT ACCEPTED TO STUDY IN NYC.

When you're faced with a decision that you're having trouble making, it helps to get your thoughts and feelings out of your head and down on paper.

Dear Diary

ON THE SET
OF ONE OF MY
FIRST TV GUEST
APPEARANCES
IN L.A. REALLY
MISSING HOME
AND FAMILY.

Lots of girls keep a diary, and I was one of them. Being able to reflect, in words, on my experiences helped me cope with them. It also gave me a safe haven to work through thoughts too private or raw to share with my girlfriends or family. Keeping a diary also makes you a friend to yourself. Diaries are helpful down the road, when you hit periods or areas of life that are difficult or confusing. They also help you realize, and celebrate, how much you've grown. In going through piles of memorabilia for this book, I came across some pages of a diary I kept when I was twenty and had just moved to Los Angeles by myself:

Starting again here in California. That's my theme for today.
And you know, starting here was more difficult than Toronto.
Or was it?

Bills are piling up each day. Lawyer to be paid off. Telephone.
My tax. Rent due, student loan, gas, electric, on & on.

Why did I ever want to grow up? Why didn't I stay in Canada?

I know I would have been happier. I think! Maybe I'm becoming gutless in my old age of twenty.

Maybe I should settle down to a normal life of security and love, responsibilities (that are not too demanding) and happiness?

I hold onto a dream—a fantasy I had when I was ten—to be a great actress. To be on the stage. The lights of Hollywood shine too bright for me and I want some protection from their glare. Something to hide under to let me escape its harshness, its hurts, and almost its come-on. That flirtatiousness that makes my hope never lose its sight.

I wonder if I know myself at all sometimes. And if I do, I can only say you are a sad person.

Worry, Worry, WORRY!...

If you ever do have the occasion to go through old diaries, one thing you might find a lot of—as I just have—is worry. "Wow," I'm thinking, "what a lot of worrying I did as a young person." Worry about grades, what I said to people, what they said to me. Well, so much for "carefree" youth.

The famous writer Mark Twain said he spent most of his life worrying about things that never happened. It's interesting to look back and see that most of my worries never *did* become realities—and if they did, not in the ways I'd imagined. It makes me wish I knew then what I know now, not so much about the concerns but about worrying in general.

Unchecked, worrying can be a pretty destructive impulse. It pulls us down by day and keeps us up at night.

The trick is knowing the difference between constructive concerns and unhelpful dark thoughts. Getting your worries out of your head and onto paper or a computer screen is a positive way to recognize what's troubling you. It also helps to remember that life is not trouble-free and that at any given moment in any person's life, many things will be up in the air.

"We would never learn to be brave or
patient, if there were only joy in the world."

—Helen Keller

Happiness.
Not!

If you're anything like I was as a teenager, you might spend a fair amount of time feeling unhappy, even when on the surface, nothing terrible has happened. Maybe you're dissatisfied with school or the neighborhood you live in, or about friendships that have faded. People see that you're unhappy and they become uncomfortable making things even worse.

With everything you've got on your plate, the constant drumbeat for happiness—whatever *that* is—can start to sound like just another of life's unrealistic demands, along with perfect exam scores and a hairless bikini line. Well, this may sound shocking, but happiness is not the be all and end all. Surprisingly enough, you'll find that low points have their place as well; they can make you reflect on things and help you grow.

So when you're not thrilled with life as you find it, at least take comfort in knowing that many great things may be accomplished through "havin' the blues." Great art, literature, and music are filled with works of sorrow and pain. For me, listening to blues artists like Billie Holiday or Etta James has always made me feel I'm not alone in whatever sadness I'm going through.

Dealing with unhappiness can also help you understand how to navigate your emotions when bad things really *do* happen. As, at some point (this being the planet Earth), they probably will.

When the Clouds **Won't Clear**

Clouds that never seem to clear can rob people of their ability to function fully. This condition is known as chronic depression, and it is often caused by an imbalance in brain chemistry. Research shows that this severe type of depression is unlikely to go away in the short term without medical treatment.

Government and nonprofit health organizations have Web sites containing information about the difference between situational depression in a well person and chronic depression related to brain chemistry. Another good source of information is www.depressedteens.com. Depression is nothing to be ashamed of. If you feel that you are suffering from symptoms of chronic depression, it is very important to talk to your parents and, together, to seek the guidance of a doctor or therapist.

When Bad Things
Do HAPPEN

Unfortunately, few (if any) of us will get through life without encountering events of staggering sadness.

My parents' breakup when I was seventeen was a very sad time for me. The world as my family had known it had come to an end. My parents could no longer pretend to be happily married. They were tired of not getting along, and the endless arguments and hurt feelings eventually became too painful. We children had to come to terms with the new arrangement.

Because my father traveled often for work, he had been absent for long stretches throughout my childhood. So, at first, the dreaded divorce wasn't as painful as my siblings and I had feared. But everything changed when my parents began to date other people. Suddenly, Dad was seeing the dental hygienist in town, and Mom was with a guy in the Air Force. They both wanted us kids to approve of their new relationships, but we couldn't comprehend our parents being with anyone but each other. I suppose hating these "strangers" made it possible to believe it was *their* fault our parents were no longer together. I also felt that I could change my parents' decision to separate by being a better daughter. It was a crushing disappointment to realize that no matter how good I tried to be or how proud they were of me, they were never getting back together.

Everyone deals differently with being sad or depressed. My way was to try to sweep it under the rug and work as hard as I could at my acting. This behavior has a name—it's called *denial*, and it will bite you in the butt sooner or later, if you don't look at what's happening and acknowledge it.

Letting Go
of **Anger**

It took several years for me to get to my anger and my feelings so I could grieve about my parents' divorce. Only after doing that could I begin to heal and find small comforts that didn't betray or deny my sense of loss. I wish I hadn't held in my feelings so long.

Here are some things you should keep in mind when you're working through a difficult time in your life:

IT'S OK TO CRY. I wish that I'd cried sooner. Bottling up my sadness only made it worse.

FEEL THE ANGER. I should have punched more pillows and really released my frustrations. That way, I could have avoided venting on myself or people around me.

REACH OUT. My siblings, girlfriends, or my parents could have been there to help me deal with my feelings, as difficult as it might have been for them. And maybe they could have used my help, too.

ALLEN JONES
BRITISH POP ARTIST
b.1937

Chapter Two

SEEING *Beauty*

Beauty takes many forms. The first step to seeing beauty in ourselves is being able to recognize beauty in the world around us. And that's not always as obvious as it seems. While everyone is trying to measure up to our consumer culture's ideas of cosmetic beauty, the truth is that there is so much *more* to see. True glamour and style are as varied and individual as we are. Wouldn't you rather live in a world where beauty can be found everywhere, including in your own mirror, than in one where it's limited to just a few places and faces?

You can develop your eye to recognize beauty beyond the usual sales banners of tastes and habits. You'll be more accepting of what you might think of as flaws, and you'll find the world a much more interesting place to look at and to be in. Most importantly, if your concept of physical beauty does not include *you*, then it is way too narrow—and you've got some work to do.

THE RELUCTANT BEAUTY QUEEN. I WAS EMBARRASSED BECAUSE I DIDN'T THINK I SHOULD HAVE WON.

Style is never simply what's trendy or what everybody else is wearing. It's about the mix—how you put it all together to express yourself. It has less to do with your money and more to do with your appetite for expression.

My style has definitely evolved over the years. My introduction came from my Mom, who created a strong sense of style on a very limited budget. One of her first jobs was in an upscale department store in Liverpool, England. On the strength of her personality and gorgeous legs, she was asked to model for the store's fashion shows. Her design heroes became Balenciaga, Chanel, Christian Dior, and Schiaparelli. I would return to these fashion icons later, but as a young girl I was being drawn in other directions. It was the beginning of the Pop Art craze, with its wild prints. I loved playing with the psychedelic paisleys and stripes, the halter tops and bell-bottoms. Next came the Women's Movement. I abandoned my bra and wore my pants zipper front and center. Then I moved to New York City, and my life and style were forever changed.

"Style is knowing who you are, what you want to say and not giving a damn."

—Gore Vidal

In New York, I was swept off my fashion feet. Diane von Furstenburg's wrap dress, Halston's lean trouser suits, and Anne Klein's sportswear were some of my favorites. The places to shop and the constant sales were staggering. Days-of-the-week panties, ponchos, kaftans, clogs, wedgies, glitter socks, hot pants, cat suits, smock tops, tube tops, and granny dresses. I wore and loved them all.

But my biggest exposure to a cross-section of fashion has to have been on *Sex and the City*, when I had the outrageous good fortune to work with Pat Field. Pat is the most amazing stylist and collaborator an actor can have, because she isn't afraid of making bold choices. Some of my favorite memories of our show were those five-hour costume fittings with Pat, where the sky was the limit for creativity. She was always encouraging me to create for myself and develop an eye for the unexpected. Pat got me to drop the "matchy-matchyness" of my fashion choices and taught me to embrace the sublime and the whimsical. The way Samantha pulled off wearing a couture Thierry Mugler suit with bangles found at a garage sale and crazy earrings from the East Village spoke volumes about Pat's wicked eye and contagious sense of fun.

Probably the best I ever felt dressed to the nines was when I wore a Herve Leger gown to the 2002 Emmy Awards. (That's me, at left, on Emmy night.) The color was right for my skin tone and hair, and the fit was sublime. When I was asked what I was wearing underneath I responded "Confidence," and I meant it. But even on the red carpet, plenty of mistakes can be made. I've found myself overwhelmed by a pouffy ball gown, unsupported in a tightly squeezed bustier, or tripping over my own train. It's easy to go too far in one direction. You don't always have to pull out all the stops.

The Teenage Brain:
A Passion for the New

Whether it's jeans big enough for three, preppy kilts, studded body parts, demure charm bracelets, nerdy spectacles, or hair in rainbow colors, teenagers don't just imitate style—in many ways they create it. In doing so, they make the world that much more interesting for the rest of us.

Some of the choices you make as a teen might be a little "too interesting" for the rest of the world. (I'm sure you've had to live through groans of "Do you *have* to wear *that* today?") Well, there are reasons why you make these choices and, believe it or not, many of the reasons have to do with what's going on between your ears.

In adolescence, the part of your brain that deals with understanding and problem solving (the cognitive pre-frontal lobe) begins to develop in new ways. This allows you to improve intellectual skills like trigonometry and calculus. It also allows you to better understand delicate changes in tone, which means the jokes get better, too. And it happens just in time. As you move out of the routines of childhood, more complex skills are needed and, trust me, you'll want the sense of humor as well as the higher math.

You're now drawn to voices outside your family and begin to find your own. This newfound perception is expressed in the friends you make, the books you read, the music you listen to, the jokes that make you laugh—and, of course, in the clothes you wear.

Who *You* Can Truly **BE!**

How do you find out what's going to look good on *you*? How do you develop your own unique style? It's easier than you think, and it starts with inspiration.

"I never thought I'd land in pictures with a face like mine."

—Audrey Hepburn

1890s   1920s   '30s   '40s   '50s   '60s

IDENTIFY WOMEN WHO HAVE BODY TYPES SIMILAR TO YOURS

Think about the message they are sending with their dress. Are their choices at odds with their body type? How are they in sync? What works? What doesn't?

EDUCATE YOURSELF ABOUT HISTORY AND TRENDS

Train your eye by looking at art, photography, and the world around you. This is what most clothing designers use as their inspiration, so why not let it be yours? If you study beauty throughout the ages, you'll open your mind to all sorts of possibilities. The notion of what's beautiful is constantly changing, so why limit your look to the current ideal?

'70s   '80s   '90s   2000...   (you.)

Know your body type like you know your blood type. The better you understand what works on your own physique, the more comfortable you'll be in whatever second skin you choose.

ALLOW YOURSELF TO EXPERIMENT

With all the thought and care that goes into creating celebrity style, it can be instructive to see what wardrobe choices your favorite celebs have made. But don't ever feel that you should slavishly follow them. There's a difference between educating yourself and blindly following high-profile style. What I love about the four women characters on *Sex and the City* is that they are all so different and yet equally celebrated.

FIND INSPIRATION IN YOUR IMAGINATION

No matter how fast your body is growing right now, there's one thing inside you that's definitely outpacing it—your imagination. What always gets mine going is reading books and plays, listening to jazz, traveling, and seeing great works of art, theater, and film. They inspire me more than any fashion magazine or red-carpet roundup.

I've always been drawn to strong female characters in literature, like *Gone with the Wind*'s Scarlett O'Hara, *Vanity Fair*'s Becky Sharp, or Shakespeare's Cleopatra. Actresses like Katharine Hepburn, Mae West, Marlene Dietrich, Carole Lombard, Ingrid Bergman, and Madeline Kahn were all unique in their talent and personal style. They continue to inspire me.

BETWEEN SETUPS AT A PHOTO SHOOT. FOR INSPIRATION, I BRING ALONG BOOKS OF MY FAVORITE PORTRAIT ARTISTS.

Through the LOOKING Glass

As an aspiring actress, I knew that my work would always involve what I look like and would, in one way or another, affect the characters I would be cast to play. Frankly, growing up, I didn't know a whole lot about cosmetics. They either caused me to break out or dried out my skin, and they were very expensive. But like it or not, it wasn't long before I came sponge-to-face, tweezers-to-brow, and wand-to-lash with professionals who were determined to turn the "girl next door" into the "starlet on the screen."

When I became a contract player for Universal Studios, I was expected to look the part. I can't really relate to the polished publicity shot you see above, on the right. I miss ME in it. But as I started to work and become better known, the pressure to look a certain way increased. The requests from agents, producers, and studios were always the same—dress sexier, let your hair grow longer, and wear more makeup.

> "It's all make-believe, isn't it?"
>
> —Marilyn Monroe

Natural Beauty

One of the most comforting moments for any actress has to be when she finally finds a makeup artist who understands the limits of her skin and whose vision complements, and even enhances, what the actress likes in herself. For me, that person is Kyra Panchenko, the makeup artist I worked with on *Sex and the City*. She really understands a natural look and, even when she's going for ultra glamour, she allows an actor's own personality to shine through.

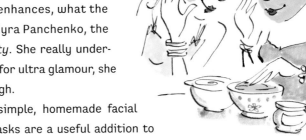

Here are a few of Kyra's recipes for simple, homemade facial masks that will help keep your skin glowing. Masks are a useful addition to your regular skin care and are a great way to relax and pamper yourself.

NOURISHING HONEY MASK

This is good for dry skin. Use a warm washcloth on your face to open the pores. Smear on a layer of honey and leave it for fifteen to thirty minutes. Rinse with warm water, then splash cold water on your face to close the pores.

STRAWBERRY YOGURT MASK

This one is good enough to eat! Yogurt will cleanse and nourish the skin, and the strawberries are full of vitamin C. Mix together one tablespoon of plain yogurt with three mashed strawberries, and spread the mixture on your face. Rinse off after five minutes.

EXFOLIATING PAPAYA MASK

The papaya will remove the buildup of dead skin, and the clay will absorb excess oils. Mix two tablespoons of mashed papaya with one tablespoon of honey and one tablespoon of rhassoul clay or fuller's earth (found in any health food store). Rinse with warm water after ten to fifteen minutes.

Professionally lit and digitally enhanced, Hollywood beauty shots are fantasy, pure and simple. Ironically, it's often the case that the more natural a photograph looks, the greater the fantasy actually is. Only the most skilled makeup artists, stylists, and lighting directors can really pull off "the natural look" convincingly. I prefer the way people (including myself) look in real life, because you have more access to their true spirit. Still...

It's fun to celebrate the artistry and imagination that goes into creating theatrical style, channeling your inner glamour-puss, and experimenting with different ways to present yourself.

WITH EACH ACTING ROLE, I FELT MORE CONFIDENT CO-CREATING A SPECIFIC LOOK AND STYLE FOR MY CHARACTER.

Skin-Care
Essentials

Most of what I have learned from Kyra is common sense. The basics are always the same. First things first: you are only as good as the night before. A good night's sleep, plenty of water, a nutritious diet, and a thorough face-cleansing regimen are key.

Before applying makeup, you must have a good skin-care routine. Make sure that the products you are using are not over-drying, clogging your pores, or irritating. Before you splurge on a whole skin-care line, ask for samples. Do the recommended patch test, putting a small amount of the product on your most sensitive skin area. If you have a bad reaction (a breakout or a rash), the product is not for you.

HERE'S A GOOD DAILY SKIN-CARE ROUTINE THAT I FOLLOW:

1. CLEANSER
Use a gentle gel cleanser geared to your specific skin type.

2. TONER
Follow with an oil-absorbing toner to remove any excess makeup and dirt.

3. MOISTURIZER
Apply a moisturizer designed for your skin type. Don't forget the sunscreen in the morning. (There are a lot of moisturizers that already contain sunscreen.) This will help prevent sun damage, which causes aging of the skin or, worse, skin cancer.

4. FACIAL SCRUB
Use a facial scrub once or twice a week to exfoliate dead skin. (If you have sensitive skin, use a nonabrasive or gentle product.)

Facing It—
Your Skin

Everyone has their beauty cross to bear, and mine has been my sensitive skin. At eighteen, I went from a clear peaches-and-cream complexion to breakouts, blackheads, cysts, and rashes that were painful—physically *and* emotionally.

The most challenging aspect of having teenage acne—and when it is chronic, it is a medical condition, not a cosmetic problem—is the shame that can be associated with it. For me, focused on a career in film and television, it was particularly troubling and, as I would soon find out, being an actress is tough on any complexion. With full makeup being applied under hot lights throughout the course of a sixteen- to eighteen-hour day, five days a week, whose skin wouldn't be challenged?

LEARNING TO SET UP AND FOLLOW A SKIN-CARE ROUTINE WAS KEY TO KEEPING MY COMPLEXION CLEAR.

In order to manage my skin, given the demands of my profession, I've learned a few lessons:

Do Not Touch!

No matter how "ready" you think your pimple looks, you'll spread the infection if you pick it, which will lengthen the life of the pimple and possibly form new ones. Picking also causes scarring. Keep your hands off your face!

Don't Irritate Your Skin

If you wear makeup, make sure that your sponges and brushes are always clean. Compacts and mascara tubes can carry bacteria and should be changed every six months. Don't share your makeup with your friends. It should be as personal as your toothbrush.

Use Drying Agents

I like the tinted kind, because you can keep the pimple clean and covered without using makeup. Apply it after washing your face in the morning and at night.

Consult a Dermatologist

Take an adult with you and go in with written questions. Ask the doctor to recommend a cleansing regimen that is easy for you to maintain. Ask about blood tests to check your hormone levels, especially your thyroid. Some skin problems have been directly linked to hypothyroidism—an easily treatable malfunction of the thyroid gland that can impair your ability to fight infections.

Don't Self-medicate

If the doctor or medication packaging says to apply or take medication twice a day, stick to that, and don't try to increase or lessen the dose or the frequency. Be patient with your body, and let your skin heal and breathe.

Know that You're Not Alone

Everyone has breakouts, even adults. I've spent many a morning in makeup trailers watching my fellow actors and their makeup artists trying to camouflage blemishes. Remember, the best part of breakouts is they don't last forever. So follow your specific regimen, use your medication—and get out of the house.

Your Best Face *Forward*

You may not want or need to wear makeup every day, but when you do, make sure you're complementing or enhancing your natural beauty—not hiding it.

FOUNDATION

Using a foundation evens out skin tone, covers up blemishes, and adds protection from the elements. For a more natural look, use a tinted moisturizer instead of a lightweight or sheer foundation. Make sure the color of your base matches your skin tone. Your face and body tones should always match. Apply foundation with a damp sponge, foundation brush, or use your fingers, and make sure you blend well beneath the jawline.

To cover any blemishes, take a tiny amount of foundation on a dry sponge and, ever so lightly, pat it onto the blemish or irritated area. Don't rub—just gently pat. Don't use a highlighter on your blemishes; it only calls attention to them.

To give the skin a healthy glow, add a bronzer. Dab it on areas where the sun would normally tan you, like the tops of your cheekbones and down the bridge of your nose.

BLUSH

Blush really pulls the look together. It gives you color and makes you look healthy and alive. Blush comes in powder, cream, or gel. Apply blush to the apples of your cheeks with your fingers or a blush brush. Keep in mind that your shade should complement your eyeshadow and lip color.

EYES

Making up your eyes takes a little more time and practice.

For a natural day look, you only need an eyelash curler, mascara, and a highlighter for under your eyes (make sure your highlighter and foundation match). I prefer the highlighter wand for its easy application and creamy texture. The undereye needs to be hydrated more than the rest of your face, so you may want to add a little eye cream to your highlighter application. When dabbing cream under your eye, use your fourth finger, which applies the least pressure.

Always curl your lashes *before* you apply your mascara. If you have blue eyes, use black or brown mascara for a more natural look. Plum or purple colors make eyes look greener. If you have brown eyes, try dark grey or dark brown mascara instead of black.

For evening, bring out the eyeshadows. I prefer creams. Your shadow should complement the colors you're wearing. First, apply the lighter shade just above the lash line using an eye brush, then take your darker shade and sweep it over the natural crease of your lid, starting from the inner corner, outward.

I recommend a soft, kohl-black pencil for your eyeliner. It's easily smudgable, and the closer you apply it to your eyelashes, the thicker they will appear.

LIPS

Lipstick, lip gloss, or lip stain? The choice is up to you. Lipsticks have the best staying power. Lip gloss looks the most natural. Lip stains give you a hint of color. Just remember to coordinate your lip color to the rest of your ensemble.

MIND over Matter

We all know that only a tiny portion of humankind will achieve supermodel stats of 5'10" and 117 pounds. But in a world saturated with images of the skinny minnies, it's easy to lose sight of what we can really expect to see in the mirror. And weight is just one issue— we also want perfect skin and teeth, hair that is glossy, bodies that are hairless, legs that are long, waists that are small, dainty feet, big eyes, pretty noses, high cheekbones, yadda, yadda, yadda. The list goes on, and it's different for every person.

It's important for us to fight unreasonable hopes and expectations about changing our looks because, according to the experts, they can lead to depression, shyness, social anxiety, and self-consciousness—not to mention eating disorders.

We've all heard "you are what you eat," and that may be true, but it has also been said that "you are what you think." Your body is an amazing instrument, and it needs love and care just like you do.

Learning to *accept* yourself as you are *right now* is key in developing and maintaining your self-esteem. It does not mean you have to be totally thrilled with everything you see or even that you can't change some of it, but feeding into unrealistic desires puts us in danger of having what no one wants: a negative body image.

When Self-Control *Gets out of* CONTROL

It's not unusual for girls to *wish* they were thinner, but using extreme tactics to control your weight can be very dangerous. Eating disorders have a variety of causes; wanting to be thinner is just one of them. Sometimes controlling your body can seem much easier than controlling the rest of your life. But remember, there is a big difference between being controlling and having self-control. Though starving yourself takes an enormous amount of determination, it is fueled by compulsive, self-destructive impulses, not by strength of will.

I witnessed this up-close when a friend in acting school spiraled down in weight to barely ninety pounds. There wasn't nearly the awareness about eating disorders then that there is now, and none of us at school could figure out what was happening to her. I was afraid she might be dying, and it was very scary and frustrating not knowing how to help. It took many years and a lot of help for my friend to finally come to terms with her issues. Today, she feels strongly about people having the courage and the information necessary to tackle eating disorders. What follows on the next page is her courageous account of a life-altering experience as she has finally come to understand it.

Sometimes controlling your body can seem much easier than controlling the rest of your life. But remember, there is a big difference between being controlling and having self-control.

A friend shares her story....

MY FRIEND JENNY. IT WAS VERY SCARY AND FRUSTRATING NOT KNOWING HOW TO HELP HER.

My eating disorders started before most people knew what eating disorders were. Now, even celebrities talk openly about them—but when I was a teenager, they were never discussed.

At seventeen, I moved from a small town to New York City to study theater. I was living in a dorm with a cafeteria and I ate to my heart's delight. I had always been thin and flat-chested, but in no time at all I filled out and came to resemble a mini Dolly Parton.

At the same time, I was discovering men. To be more precise, men were discovering me. Whereas only months before they had treated me as a child, now they seemed to be coming out of the woodwork. It was all pretty exciting but also scary and confusing. I wasn't ready for all this womanly attention. But this wasn't the only issue. I had not been accepted back for my second year at theater school, which was a devastating blow to my self-confidence.

My mother, who was thin but always weight-conscious and openly repulsed by body fat, began constantly nagging me about my weight gain. Unhappy with myself and in over my head, I became totally overwhelmed. I decided to lose weight. At 5' 3" and 118 pounds, I should have gone safely down to around 110, but as the extra pounds fell away, I got so excited about how successful I was that I just kept going. Food was the one place I had power and control—and let me tell you, it was an addictive high. I continued to starve myself for the next three years and went down to a mere eighty-seven pounds.

Then came the binging and purging, which lasted another seven years. I lived on practically nothing, going to auditions, working in restaurants, while spending up to five hundred dollars a week that I would steal out of my boyfriend's pockets so I could buy junk food, eat it, and then throw up. I would be in a doctor's office at least once a week during this time—fainting spells, heart palpitations, no periods, hair loss, and then my teeth started to rot. I couldn't hide what I'd become, and I didn't look or feel like a young woman of twenty-nine.

With the support of a loving friend, with whom I decided to share my years of self-abuse, I found a trained therapist so I could start to understand what was at the root of my behavior. It had to do with my self-esteem, which was all mixed up in my looks and body image. Reaching out for help was the first step to changing this vicious cycle. It's a condition that I live with to this day, and the best way to guard against it is to take care of myself emotionally and physically.

Food for Thought

Good eating habits, like good exercise, will serve you for the rest of your life. Taking care to eat a balanced diet will decrease your chances of getting sick. Eating fresh, nutritious food is a message to your body that you care about yourself. I discovered cooking in my late teens, and it has become one of my favorite hobbies. Food is a world unto itself, rich with history, cultural interest—and tastes, all worth trying at least once.

A well-prepared meal is one of the greatest things life has to offer. Cheap fast-food fixes in my fuel tank just won't do. Good food gives me the energy to do whatever I set my mind to. Although a busy schedule sometimes makes it hard to eat well, I make it a priority.

Moving Targets

A rolling stone gathers no moss—or fat, for that matter. Exercising takes a bit more commitment than eating well, but the rewards are enormous. First of all, it's one of the best ways to reduce stress.

I exercise at least three times a week with a strong cardio workout and light weights. But you don't have to sweat it out in a gym for hours. Just a twenty-minute brisk walk can do wonders, clearing the mind and keeping you healthy. You can also try yoga, pilates, or kickboxing. Even skipping rope or dance classes are great ways to improve fitness and relaxation. Whatever exercise you choose, make sure it's something you enjoy. Don't sign up for six months' worth of classes before you've gone a few times and know it's right for you. Exercise should be fun as well as effective—whatever your goal is.

Physical activity gets your blood flowing, moves toxins out of your system, and encourages your body to produce endorphins and other mood-elevating chemicals. Being physically fit not only makes you look better, it also gives you a better outlook on life.

Sweet Dreams

Probably nothing on Earth—no product you buy, diet you might endure, or haircut you pay for—will ever have a more positive effect on your overall appearance and well-being than getting enough rest.

Of course, there are plenty of times when looking good is worth sacrificing for something even better, like a great adventure or an unforgettable meal, but that won't wreak much havoc on your looks if you're generally eating and sleeping well.

There's no beauty remedy better for your skin, eyes, belly, even hair, than a good night's rest.

Unfortunately, with the rough schedule many of us have, it can be tough to get long periods of rest. You really have to try to make it a priority.

My own schedule sometimes throws my routine off-kilter but, over the years, I've become pretty good at power-napping, just to grab five minutes of rest. My most tried-and-true method of getting to sleep when I'm all pumped up is to start at the top of my head and move all the way down to my toes, slowly tensing and then releasing my muscles and taking deep, long breaths at the same time. (I usually drop off before I even get to my knees.) It's like checking in with all parts of your body and shutting them down one after the other.

The Teenage Brain:
The Scoop on Sleep

Here's some handy scientific info you might want to show your parents: there is a bona fide *biological* explanation for why you might want to blow curfew and then sleep until noon.

Teenagers, recent studies tell us, have night-owl brains. Scientists focusing on sleep cycles have determined that the onset of adolescence brings with it an actual "phase delay" in terms of the way sleep-inducing brain chemicals (melatonin and others) flow into and out of your system. For teens, the chemicals arrive later and last well into the morning, feeding the temptation to stay up late and then snooze through the alarm.

Fascinating, but what gives? Doesn't your brain know that class starts at 8:00 A.M. and your mom likes to see you in bunny slippers and pjs by 10:00 P.M.? Well, it seems that evolution had other ideas.

In almost all areas of the animal kingdom, adolescence is a crucial time for striking out and forming bonds. Late-night activity frees adolescents from parental rule. Basically, it's about the only time of day when the young guns can strut their stuff without driving the authority figures crazy. Some scholars also believe that, back when we were all living in caves, strong young adults may have been required to keep watch while the very young and the old folks dozed. See, Dad? It's all for *your* protection!

"I don't want you to cover your bases. I want you to reach for your dreams."

—My Dad, when I considered taking typing instead of drama in high school

LEFT: ME AT SIX, HOLDING MY BABY BROTHER, CHRIS. **ABOVE:** DISPLAYING OUR CATCH FROM MY DAD'S ONE AND ONLY FISHING TRIP. (THAT'S ME ON THE LEFT.)

Chapter Three

WE ARE *Family*

Families are as unique as snowflakes, even the happy ones. And they can be just as hard as snowflakes to pin down. Just when you think you've learned how to handle them, something happens, and the whole pretty picture melts before your eyes.

There are all sorts of ways families may not fit the traditional mold. But families that don't conform to stereotypes can still make you proud of them—and of yourself, for the special skills you've learned in a non-traditional situation.

My family was different from others I knew growing up, partly because we were immigrants. Both of my parents are from Liverpool, England, and although they spoke English, with their accents they certainly didn't sound like anyone else we met on rural Vancouver Island (on Canada's west coast). Money was always scarce. Not just for extras like allowances or family vacations, but for essentials like central heating or a reliable car. Although we were clothed and fed, we were always one step away from not being able to pay the bills.

My Dad had trained as a construction engineer, and he was "handy," so he built our house mostly out of extra building material from his various job sites. Needless to say, our home and yard were constantly under construction for most of my childhood.

Dad had terrible luck with the used cars we could afford and resorted to buying similar models from junkyards for parts, from which he'd create a "new" car, leaving behind an assembly line of auto carcasses in our backyard. Going for a drive, you never knew if ol' "Frankencar" was going to make it or if you'd have to get out and give it a push.

I have always loved my family. Maybe because we were "different," we knew how to pull together. Somehow money could always be found for whatever interests we wanted to pursue, as long as we were committed to them.

LEFT: CELEBRATING MY SISTER CHERRY'S 17TH BIRTHDAY, 1971.
ABOVE: MY PARENTS, NOW AS FRIENDS, 1992.

Gotta Love **the 'Rents**

There are bound to be ups and downs, and you won't always get what you want. But like any other relationship, you can improve it by communicating and by treating each other with respect.

VISITING HOME AT 21. SEEING MY PARENTS AS INDIVIDUALS, NOT JUST AS MY MOM AND DAD.

When I was little, I cried when my parents left the room. As a teen, I couldn't get them out of my room fast enough. For years it may seem that if your mom and dad aren't telling you what to do, they're embarrassing you in public. You want to be independent, try new things, and make your own decisions. Your parents want to protect you, educate you, and see you make sensible choices. The reason it feels like you're coming from two different places is because you *are*. While you are busy sampling all life has to offer, they are determined to point out all the dangers you might face.

We tend to overlook the fact that our parents can be vulnerable, too. As a young woman, I was so wrapped up in a romanticized myth of my parents that it took me a very long time to see them as people with their own attributes, fears, and flaws. After all, you don't need a diploma or degree to become a parent. Biological equipment is all that's required. The rest is the luck of the draw.

Some parents have a better understanding of their role in bringing up children than others. What I have learned is to be thankful for what my parents were able to give me growing up, because I believe they did the best they could with what they had.

Try to see where your parents are coming from.

And try to gain some perspective on your own situation. One way to do that is to learn about the forces that affect you. Knowledge is power! The brain is the master-control center for thoughts and feelings. How the brain functions has a *huge* influence on how one experiences the world.

Teenage brains are...well, different. Knowing how they're different can help you understand yourself better and help better explain YOU to the rest of the world.

The Teenage Brain:
A Rollercoaster Ride

Do you feel like you're thinking too much, feeling too deeply, and seeing more than ever before? Well, groundbreaking new research reveals that as a teenager you are, in fact, very likely to be experiencing life more vibrantly than you ever did as a child or will again as an adult.

But why?

It turns out that, just as you are trying to figure out a whole bunch of new stuff (boys, fashion, sex, peer pressure), the chemistry *and even the size* of your brain changes (it gets bigger) to allow a supercharged period of development.

Between the ages of thirteen and twenty, hormonal tides and neurological charges in teenage brains reward the quest for new ideas and bright horizons, basically making you want to stay up late and take risks. It isn't until sometime in your mid-twenties that the brain settles down and shrinks back to its ho-hum, business-as-usual size. It also isn't until then that the part of your brain associated with "policing" the whole party (the pre-frontal cortex) reaches its full development. Sorry, but it remains rather puny until you're entirely grown up.

Like a thrilling rollercoaster ride, this time of heightened new experience can be a challenge to navigate. The ramped-up intensity of your feelings at this time can also make minor annoyances—guys teasing, Mom singing, Dad sneezing—intolerable. There's also the danger that in your exuberance, you may unwittingly put yourself in harm's way. What does this all mean? The teenage brain is cause for celebration—and for caution.

The *Romance* of Risk

I'VE ALWAYS BEEN A RISK-TAKER.

Not by throwing myself out of planes or that sort of thing, but by putting myself in situations and circumstances where I didn't know whether I'd be up to the challenge.

Following your dream can be like that— you don't know whether you'll be smart enough or talented enough or lucky enough to do what you want to do. When there are so many others who want the same career as you, there's always the looming question: Will you be good enough?

The biggest risk I ever took was moving to New York by myself at the age of sixteen. I had graduated from high school early and been accepted to a theater school some 3,000 miles away. My hometown had a population of just under 5,000 people. The population of New York City at that time was over *five million*, and I didn't know a single person there.

My grandmother had been involved with the Salvation Army, and my parents felt very secure about me living at a place run by them. I picked the Parkside Evangeline Women's Residence because it was within walking distance of my school and overlooked a small park in Gramercy Place.

The night before I got on the plane, I remember crying with my best friend because I wasn't sure I wanted to leave. Then I had a fight with my boyfriend because he didn't want me to go. On top of everything, my father had insisted that I get a perm before I left because, as he put it, I was "not only representing the family," I was "representing Canada." Not too much pressure!

The biggest risk I ever took was moving to New York
by myself at the age of sixteen.

When I finally arrived in New York after traveling for fifteen hours and having trouble with the immigration officer (my school visa was incomplete), it was pouring rain. I got *drenched*, and my new perm began to smell like rotten eggs. So there I was: my one suitcase, filled mostly with books, was so heavy I could barely carry it; my hair was fried; and the city smelled like poop. When I finally checked into my tiny room at the women's residence, the first thing I did was lie down on the bed and cry my eyes out.

But the next day was totally amazing. It was 1973, and it had just been announced that the Vietnam War was ending. All the bells in New York City started ringing in celebration. The residence, it turned out, overlooked not just any small park, but Gramercy Park, one of the quaintest spots in the whole city. The sun had come out, and the whole place was transformed. I remember calling home collect and telling them that I had made it safely, and all the bells were ringing. I'll never forget what my Dad said: "Honey, the bells are ringing for you."

Next, I walked to 31st Street and Madison Avenue to my school, the American Academy of Dramatic Arts, and peeked through the glass doors. I was so thrilled to see it; this was my dream, the culmination of everything I had hoped for. It was a great moment. Still, I was so homesick the first few weeks, I didn't know if I'd make it through the first semester.

What made me take that risk? I guess I felt I was ready to test myself at another level and see what I could learn and whether or not I could keep up. Most importantly, I needed to find out whether the performing arts were where I belonged. I worked my butt off at that school and was accepted for a second year. Now, I feel lucky that I've been able to work ever since in a profession that I love. This was a risk worth taking and, interestingly enough, one that my rather conservative parents always supported. I suppose they understood how much it meant to me.

> I worked my butt off at theater school and was accepted for a second year. Now, I feel lucky that I've been able to work ever since in a profession that I love. This was a risk worth taking.

WINNING THE GOLDEN GLOBE FOR *SEX AND THE CITY.*

69

But I can also remember risks that were **NOT** worth taking....

The *Sneak*-Out

My Mom and I had our first big clash when I was thirteen. Living in a small town, without a lot of places to meet and hang out, my girlfriend and I decided to sneak out to a weekend beach party.

At around 1:00 A.M., long after my Mom had fallen asleep, my friend and her older boyfriend picked me up in his new Mazda coupe. No one heard us as we drove off to the beach and the now-dwindling party, where my friend's boyfriend proceeded to finish off a good portion of the remaining beer.

After staying for over an hour, we got back in the car and drove around. As we were speeding along the winding back roads at 3:00 A.M., I remember sitting in the back seat trying to calculate just how many beers my friend's boyfriend might have had. Neither my friend nor I could drive, so we couldn't take over the wheel.

MY MOM WASN'T ALWAYS TOUGH ON ME. IT JUST SEEMED THAT WAY AT THE TIME.

What if he'd had too many drinks?
What if we got into an accident or were stopped by the cops?
What would my friends think if I asked them to stop the car?
Who would I call to pick me up?

70

If I didn't get a ride, I'd have to walk home by myself in the dark for over eight miles. How long would that take me? My Mom would certainly be up by then, and all hell would break loose. I had never felt so scared, because I couldn't find a way out.

I did get home, after finally speaking up and telling my friend I'd had enough. They dropped me off at the end of my street around 4:00 A.M., and I ran to the house and sneaked back in through the kitchen—where my mother was waiting for me. She was furious. She had called the police, whom she promptly phoned again now that I was back. When the officer arrived, he asked whether I'd been drinking (I hadn't), and he told me that I could be put away in a detention home if I ever did something like this again. I was humiliated, but little did they know their threat was nowhere near as frightening as being a passenger in the Mazda coupe with a drunk driver at the wheel. I had risked my life without thinking it through.

This experience affected me then and has stuck with me to this day. A big reason is because, a year later, a school friend of mine died in a car accident where drinking was a factor. I remember thinking that it could have easily been me. I continue to treat drugs and alcohol with caution and treat myself with the utmost respect.

Biology Check: Why We Fight

Anyone who has had PMS (Pre-menstrual Syndrome) knows the power of mood-altering hormones—and like it or not, for the next several years you'll be awash in them. Add to this stew the fact that there's a lot of stuff driving you crazy: your skin has broken out, you've gained ten pounds in the last six months, and your so-called boyfriend just told you how cute your best friend is. Although your parents or siblings may very well be the most annoying people on Earth, be aware that you might also be operating with a particularly short fuse—thanks to hormone surges.

BATHING BEAUTIES OF 1958. MY SISTER CHERRY, AT LEFT, AND ME.

THICKER than Water

Whether you're more likely to wage a war of the worlds than experience a Vulcan mind meld with your sibs, the intimacy of your relationship with your brothers and sisters will have an impact on you throughout your life. Sisters and brothers understand what it's like to live in your house and grow up with your parents. But since they're not *you*, they may be able to give you a slightly different perspective on things.

I have two sisters and a younger brother. Growing up, I adored my big sister. She was two years and two months older and my idol. She was beautiful, smart, and shy—the complete opposite of me: chubby, overactive, and ready to take on the world. She was very petite and girly growing up, before turning super sexy in high school. (I remember when she wore a clingy black halter dress to graduation that made her look exactly like Cher, who was insanely popular at the time.) I was more of a tomboy, and my role in the family was to be the clown, the entertainer. I loved to make everyone laugh so we could change the subject, especially when conflicts arose. My Dad called me The Red Herring because I could so craftily shift the direction of a conversation.

Although we got along, my older sister and I were not always chummy. When she became a teenager, I was still a tween, and she thought I was a "dink" (the lowest of the low) who was not worth talking to. I remember her throwing stones at me to clear off as she and her friends sat around being cool and listening to Beatles records.

Our father encouraged a competitive climate among his kids. Looking back, I wish that our differences had been more openly acknowledged and celebrated instead of used as a measuring stick for attention and affection. My Dad was raised that way. He had been a talented young athlete who dreamed of running the world's first four-minute mile, and his father had instilled in him a critical view of his skills so he'd try harder.

None of us kids responded well to my Dad's "good intentions." We were all so incredibly different in personality, age, and development and all gifted in our own unique ways.

What works for one child doesn't necessarily work for another. Genuine self-esteem isn't about competing or comparing yourself to anyone.

LOOKING UP:
Teachers and Mentors

They're close to you, but not too close—people who know you now, but didn't when you were teething. You're even willing to admit that, unlike your parents, they might actually know a thing or two. Although it may be hard to imagine, your teachers, coaches, and even great-aunts have all been teenagers. Even though it may have been in the Dark Ages— waaaaaay before the iPod—maybe they have something valuable they can share with you about how they dealt with challenges as a teenager. Why not ask them?

    I was lucky to have had strong role models early in my life. My great-aunt in Liverpool was one. We had met during a family vacation, and then I lived with her while attending school in Liverpool when I was eleven and twelve. She was a teacher and had many interests in the theater, arts, and literature. She encouraged me to read plays and poetry and to paint with watercolors. She was terribly bossy and strict and demanded a lot from me. She always maintained that she only asked what she felt I was capable of, and her demands, as much as I feared them, were always a clear message to me that she had great confidence in me and my talent.

"Your family thinks of you as a pet; you have to leave them. They are just where you came from; they are not what you are. They will give you everything they have, but that will not make you want it, or know what to do with it. Wanting some other way to live is proof enough of deserving it."

—Lillian Hellman

It's easy to overlook the value of your family while you're still living at home and dealing with the daily frictions of living together. Once you head out on your own, you'll see that your family has played a huge role in making you the person you are. Leaving the protective circle of your family will also make you realize what invaluable, self-defining assets friends are in your life. Just about every hero's journey—Wendy's in *Peter Pan*, Dorothy's in *The Wonderful Wizard of Oz*, or Frodo's in *The Lord of the Rings*—begins with the hero leaving home and finding new guides.

MY CLOSEST HIGH SCHOOL PAL, JACKIE WEST, AND ME.

As we venture out of the universe of our families, choosing friends is one of the most critical ways in which we find a new family, one that we create for ourselves.

"A good friend is one who thinks that you are a good egg, even though she knows you're slightly cracked."

—Anonymous

Chapter Four

BETWEEN *Friends*

When women talk or write to me about what they love most about *Sex and the City*, they always touch on the same thing. It isn't the sex, it isn't the city, and it certainly isn't the shoes. It's the thrill they get from watching four grown women spend time together—giving and getting daily counsel on everything from the sublime date to the ridiculous argument. The truth is, once school ends and our peer groups no longer organize our lives, opportunities to hang with girlfriends aren't as easy to come by as they once were. Daily access to girlfriends is something most women beyond school age dearly miss.

Girlfriends are your support teams, fashion advisers, life coaches, shoulders to cry on, cheerleaders, and so much more. The bonds you form as young women can last a lifetime—or not. It almost doesn't matter. What *does* matter is the love that you show and the care that you take with each other *now*. This laughter and friendship will sustain and nurture you for many years to come.

SOMETIMES YOU HIT GIRLFRIEND GOLD.

My best friend growing up was Jackie West. We were quite different—she was academic, I was artistic—but in our drive and passion for learning, we recognized we were kindred spirits. Jackie supported my dream of becoming an actress and helped me get through my academic requirements so I could graduate early. I made her laugh and encouraged her not to take her boyfriend troubles so seriously.

We have always been there for each another—and continue to be, despite the years and the physical distance between us.

Girlfriends, Girlfriends!

LEFT: JACKIE AND ME, SUMMER 1998.
RIGHT: JEN AND ME IN OUR 20s.
TAKEN IN A STATION PHOTO BOOTH.

But I was also lucky because, in terms of meeting great girlfriends, my move to New York City turned out to be a very rich experience. My second day at theater school, I met my lifelong best friend, Jen Gelfer, a tough, savvy New Yorker. Jen taught me the difference between uptown and downtown (I was so green) and was my guide to the best of NYC. Her parents invited me to holiday dinners and for weekends, and I soon became part of the family. Without Jen and her family's care and acceptance, it would have been a much lonelier time for me. Jen and I are still the best of friends, and we continue to work together, collaborating on theater productions and film projects.

After three months at the Salvation Army residence and in various sublets, I was lucky enough to be accepted at The Rehearsal Club—an old brownstone right next door to the Museum of Modern Art on 53rd Street. The Club rented rooms to young women in the performing arts for close to nothing. It was a legendary New York establishment. The 1930s movie *Stage Door* was based on it, and it had famous alumnae, including Carol Burnett, Blythe Danner, and Sandy Duncan.

After passing a mandatory audition, I was given a room. The Club housed about twenty girls—actresses, singers, dancers, and even some high-stepping Rockettes from Radio City Music Hall. Most were studying at various performing arts institutions around town. For fifty bucks a week, you shared a room and got three meals a day. No one had a private phone or answering machine—and the public phone in the lobby had a strict time limit. We all took turns doing phone duty, fridge cleanup, and answering the front door. When men called on us for dates, they were never allowed beyond the front parlor. It was like something out of Jane Austen.

It was wonderful to be surrounded by all these young women pursuing the same dream.

I felt like I belonged and quickly formed friendships and a strong support network. If one girl got an audition for a commercial, we'd all pull for her to get a callback. If someone landed a role in a show, on Broadway or off, we'd cheer her on during the previews. I landed my first film role while I was living there, and we all celebrated. Former New York City mayor John Lindsay played my father in the film and we became friends. The girls on phone duty swooned whenever he called.

Living with other young women from all over the country was an unforgettable bonding experience that I still treasure. We were all up against tough odds. It helped a lot to feel the support of the other girls.

Trouble in Paradise

Friendships become such a huge part of our lives and identity that it can seriously rock our world when they change—especially when we're not expecting it. But friendships grow and branch out and sometimes wither.

Learning how to adapt to their cycles will help you weather these changes. Here are some of the things that I've witnessed among friends, and some thoughts on how to cope when these things happen to you.

Three's a crowd

a crowd
a crowd
a crowd

So your old best friend has a new best friend, and you're a little hurt. Don't run away mad. Try to accept your friend's new interests. And could it be that it's time for you to widen your perspective as well? Being flexible will help you grow. All relationships ebb and flow, as people adapt to new situations and discover new things about themselves and the people around them. In friendship, *quality*, not quantity, is what counts. And hanging out with a variety of buddies—think of Samantha, Carrie, Miranda, and Charlotte—brings variety and diversity to your life.

ENVY,
the green-eyed
MONSTER

It's not very attractive, but everyone feels it at one time or another. Still, feeling envy is tough to admit. We hate letting people know that we might feel less than adequate or that someone else is better than we are. The situation is even harder to bear when we find we've become envious of a close friend. Being a friend means more than having, or lending, a shoulder to cry on. It also means being able to share in each other's joys and successes. It sounds so simple. It isn't always.

You love your best friend like crazy, but you hate it when she gets all the male attention, does better than you in school, flaunts the trendy jeans you can't afford, or looks great in a bathing suit while doing a back flip off the high-board. You know that you should be happy for her, but sometimes it all just seems *so* unfair.

Feeling envious of someone else's accomplishments tells you that you, too, want to excel in some way. By challenging yourself and understanding your own strengths, you will be able to make that happen.

Even if your gifts and talents are not as obvious or spectacular as those you see in your friend, I guarantee you, they are infinitely more important to you. In fact, they are all that matters.

If you feel pangs of envy, let them motivate you to uncover and develop your own resources for success. Then, genuinely celebrate the fact that you have such an extraordinary friend. Nurture yourself and protect your ability to enjoy openheartedly the good fortune of others. It's one of your great natural gifts.

81

She grills
YOU, but she never
opens up

She gets you to talk about your problems, but she never tells you hers. People who continually get you to dwell on your problems are like parasites, swelling in self-importance with each compromising confidence you divulge. You feel drained because you *have* been drained. If this relationship is important to you, level with your girlfriend and let her know friendship is a two-way street where both parties let down their hair and get to know each other.

It's ALL about HER

HER HER

Your closest girlfriend talks about herself all the time, but seems to lose interest whenever the conversation turns to you. Unfortunately, not everyone has mastered the fine art of listening—one of the most important social skills you can develop. It not only makes you more compassionate, it also gives you the opportunity to learn from others.

Think about your friend. Is she talking nervously all the time just to avoid (heaven forbid) an awkward silence? Is she really disinterested in you, or is she just unable to slow down long enough to give you enough space to open up? Does she understand that you actually are willing to share yourself with her?

If you value the friendship, let her know you need a little more air space to let your thoughts and feelings surface. Tell her that there are things you'd like to share with her, but they just don't come tumbling out of you. If she responds with interest, give her a chance. If she looks burdened by the whole thing, then maybe it really *is* all about her. It could be time to move on.

When a boyfriend enters the scene

Now one of you has a boyfriend. How do you share time? This is always a tough one and, oh, so familiar. If you're not super careful, you may find yourself missing appointments, breaking dates with your girlfriends, and being late for everything in order to be with your guy. You may, in fact, miss your friends dearly, but while you're pining away in silence, they might be simmering at every perceived slight. Eventually, they may even lash out at you with what may seem an unduly harsh attack. No one is really wrong, but everyone feels badly. How can this be avoided? With care.

If you are the one with the boyfriend, do not let anything or anyone make you give up your girlfriends. Make time for them, and don't let "the guy" become the center of your life. Believe me, men will come and go but strong girlfriend bonds are forever.

If it's your friend who seems to have forsaken you for a new beau, try to be tolerant. Understand that she is probably caught up in the moment and is struggling just to keep her act together. She hasn't forgotten you and probably needs you more than ever. Be direct with her when you feel she's been careless with you and don't let your anger build up.

BOYFRIEND *theft*

Seeing the same people every day has its joys and its perils. You and your best friend have so many similar points of reference that not only do you go for the same guys but the same guys go for you. Suddenly, the two people you enjoyed most in the world are enjoying each other a little too much—and you now find three's a crowd.

The old saying "All is fair in love and war" is kind of brutal, but there's some truth to how well it describes human behavior. I am not saying that you should excuse a betrayal; I'm just suggesting that you're not alone in this, and that you can survive it.

The best thing for all concerned is to give each other as much distance as possible, and try to be as sensitive to each other as you can. Even if you can't stand each other at the moment, don't do or say anything you know you'll regret later. With everything you have in common, it's not unthinkable that someday you might want to be friends again.

Also remember that, even if your friend *did* act like a snake in the grass, it is basically impossible to steal someone away who doesn't want to be stolen. Though you're sure to be hurt now, you probably didn't lose as much as you might think.

Fitting **IN**

Physically, I was a late bloomer, which made it difficult for me to feel like I fit in with my peers. Compounding the matter, I had skipped a grade, so everyone in my class was a year older than I was and, naturally, more physically developed. A year in a teenager's life can seem forever. I felt like a child next to the older girls sporting bras and carrying packs of tampons. I remember changing for gym class in the toilet cubicle, hiding so no one could see my childlike body. I became the topic of gossip.

Having an older sister made me even more eager to grow up and do all the cool things she was allowed to do, like wear makeup, shave her legs, and date boys. Eventually my body did catch up, but those years of feeling like an odd duck had their impact—and maybe it was not entirely negative. Between being an immigrant, growing up poor, and moving around a lot, over the years I developed a bit of an outsider mentality. I think that has helped me take some of the risks I've needed to take as an actress.

THE AWKWARD YEARS BETWEEN CHILD AND TEEN.
TOP. (FROM LEFT): ALMOST 12; FIRST YEAR OF JUNIOR HIGH SCHOOL, 13.
BOTTOM. (FROM LEFT): 14 YEARS OLD; 15 AND ON TO SENIOR HIGH.

There's a certain freedom that comes with knowing you can survive because you've been on your own before.

MEAN Girls

Even rugged individualists are not immune to the joy of belonging, but if you're giving up your self-respect, your principles, or your integrity to do what other people think you should do, the price you're paying for going along with the group is too high.

Sometimes groups of girls move from being friendly individuals enjoying each other's company to behaving like queen bees ruling a hive. Suddenly, the group you feel most comfortable hanging out with inexplicably morphs into a clique where no one gets in—and no one gets out—without paying a heavy emotional price.

How will you know when, or if, your pals have crossed the line? Look for the following signs:

- **Your group insists on approving all your social choices.**
- **Your group has targeted someone for ridicule.**
- **A set number of girls must be maintained in your group. A new person can be admitted only when someone else gets kicked out.**
- **Your friends have rules regarding clothing, hairstyles, or lunch room/hallway conduct that must be followed.**
- **Those who don't follow the rules are punished in some agreed-upon way.**
- **Group discussions revolve around gossip.**

If this is happening in your group, you might want to kick yourself out and look for some new friends. Be aware that this may make you the subject of the group's gossip or ridicule. You'll need to find strength in your own convictions in order to move on.

Games People
PLAY

I attended school in Liverpool at eleven, came back to Canada for junior high school at twelve, on to New York at sixteen, got my first professional film role at seventeen, first professional theater job at eighteen and then moved to Los Angeles at twenty. Phew! Between all the travel and hours of training, I guess I just never cared enough about being a big social success to notice whatever lethal cliques might be developing around me. Sadly, however, I can report that toxic cliques do not end in school. In my adult life, I have witnessed an alarming amount of this disturbing social dynamic. In social and professional circles of power and influence, the queen-bee mentality is alive and kicking. (Think high school, with money.) And, yes, even a celebrity can find herself the odd girl out when a clique forms on set.

For the most part, laughter, real friends, and moving on are the best medicine.

DON'T FORGET TO KEEP YOUR SENSE OF HUMOR HANDY.

89

Toxic *Talk*...

As someone who lives in the public eye, I know more about gossip than I ever wanted to. Gossip is hurtful, damaging, and rarely contains even the smallest grain of truth. So why do so many people have such a huge appetite for it? It's kind of like eating junk food—no nutrition, a huge rush, and an energy crash. Gossip persists because everyone wants to be "in the know."

I once saw the play *Doubt* by John Patrick Shanley, and in it a character describes gossip as being like a feather pillow taken to a rooftop and shredded with a knife. The feathers are scattered everywhere, of course—blown by the wind, never to be put back inside. Gossip is like that. Even when it's proven wrong, the mess it makes can be irreversible and therefore deeply wounding. It's natural to want to know and understand the behavior of people around you, with whom you share the world, but try to distinguish between information and gossip. And remember that if someone gossips *with* you, they're also likely to gossip *about* you.

...and Bullies

Bullying is more than just teasing. It can take the form of name-calling, intimidation, spreading rumors, sending harassing or backbiting emails or texts, taking someone else's stuff, as well as physical aggression like pushing, shoving, or hitting. Bullies typically feel inadequate, ugly, or weak in some critical way and gain a perverse sense of power and control by making other people suffer. I once knew someone who had come to rely on bullying as a crutch so much that she actually had to leave little yellow sticky notes around her workspace to remind herself to "be good to others." At least she was working on it.

The worst kind of bully is what experts identify as the "undercover" type. Perhaps you've met one, too. Maybe you even thought he or she was your friend. This person is Miss or Mr. Congeniality on the surface but, unfortunately, you know better. Undercover bullies are the most poisonous of all because they are the hardest to spot.

HERE ARE SOME STRATEGIES YOU CAN USE TO KEEP BULLIES FROM GETTING THE BEST OF YOU.

TELL SOMEONE IN AUTHORITY

Sometimes it seems wiser to suffer in silence. Maybe you think the nightmare will only get worse if you report it. But it's important that friends, parents, bosses, coaches, or sometimes even law enforcement officials (in serious cases, such as threats of bodily harm) are aware when you are being harassed, so you can work together to end it. **Keeping the bullying a secret only ensures that it will continue.**

STRENGTH IN NUMBERS

Real friends back each other up if a bully tries to single out one of you for personal attention. If you present a united front and refuse to be intimidated, a bully will usually move on to easier prey.

DO NOT RETALIATE

Maybe you'd feel better in the short term if you gave your tormentor a taste of his or her own medicine. But is that the kind of person you really want to be? And, much of the time, what undercover bullies want most is to get a rise out of you and see you make a fool of yourself. Don't give them the satisfaction. Most bullies will give up if you don't react the way they want when they provoke you.

SAMANTHA WOULDN'T PUT UP WITH BS, AND NEITHER SHOULD YOU.

"If it has tires or testicles, you're going to have trouble with it."

—comedienne Linda Firney

Chapter Five

ALL THE YOUNG

GUYS. Mysterious? Challenging? Annoying? Aliens? Or just another group of humans dealing with changes—like you? Guys are as susceptible as we are to peer pressure, gossip, and the pursuit of media perfection. And while we know they didn't actually fly in from another planet, guys *do* differ from girls in some pretty significant ways. Sometimes it helps to look at how those differences play out.

MY JUNIOR HIGH SCHOOL BASKETBALL TEAM: THE COMOX TIGERS. *Grrrrrr...*

The Teenage Brain:
The Emotional Divide

We've all been there—you're so excited to get a call from your first boyfriend, but the conversation is, well, let's just say your new sweetie is no Shakespeare on the phone. How can a guy who seems so smart have so little to say? What is *up* with this?

Well, it appears there are reasons. Not only is there a social expectation for guys to be strong and silent, but there is also scientific evidence that boys are less likely to understand their emotions and are therefore less able to express them. Part of it has to do with wiring.

Within a girl's brain, a lot more sharing goes on between the right and left hemispheres. This means that emotions registering on one side of the brain are partially processed on the other side where logic, reasoning, and language are centered. In a boy's brain, however, there is less back-and-forth between the hemispheres. Emotion and language lie on either side of a divide.

While girls are accustomed to sharing every little thing with each other, guys (who feel emotions just as deeply) are not. It's not until they are older and have more experience and maturity that they become better equipped to put words to their feelings. And there's more.

It seems that girls' brains mature much faster than boys' on a steady curve from age thirteen to seventeen. It isn't until the age of eighteen to twenty-four that boys actually catch up. That doesn't mean that girls are smarter than boys at any point, but during the teen years, the rapidly maturing and more integrated brains of girls allow them to navigate their emotions through language more effectively.

IMPORTANT FRIENDSHIP REMINDER
Don't neglect your girlfriends just because you have a boyfriend. Remember, if you can't find time to spend with them—call!

Who's the Boss?
The Unpredictable Organ

Imagine that you had a body part with a mind of its own. Imagine that this body part did whatever it wanted, wherever it wanted, whenever it wanted. Now imagine that this body part had the power to humiliate you in class, in front of your parents, or when you're hanging out with someone you like. Then imagine feeling as though you had to skip doing things you wanted to do because the body part was so unpredictable. You'd wonder who was really in charge: you or the body part.

This unsettling scenario is what many young men go through as their bodies mature sexually. Just as girls' bodies are changing in very visible ways, boys' bodies are changing dramatically, too. As excruciating as it is to have people around you checking out the size of your chest, at least your chest size isn't changing several times a day!

If the guys you know seem confused, preoccupied, or are sending out mixed messages, keep in mind that they may be struggling just to hold down the fort! Don't despair. It gets better.... Honestly.

Boys' early attempts at romance have a big impact on us as girls. And at some level, as we grow up, we continue to believe that the confounding behavior of adolescent boys is just the way guys are—forever. It takes many of us a long time to recognize that that's just not true. Boys *do* grow into men, they do gain control over their bodies (well, sort of), and someday they will be capable of letting you know exactly how they feel about you. If you get mixed signals from guys going through puberty, be patient and don't write them off (the guys, not the signals). They may just be overwhelmed.

MICHELANGELO
David
1501-4

DATING DATING DATING
(aka Getting to Know You)

It's not uncommon to get swept up in the fantasy of the moment, but take your time. Dating can feel like an audition, but it can also be fun. It's a ritual of sorts. And like buying a new outfit, a new shade of lipstick, or parting your hair a different way, having a guy pick you up at home and take you out can make you feel kinda special.

More importantly, dating gives you an opportunity to find out what you and this other person have in common and how you differ. It allows you to see him in different situations at different times and to figure out who he truly is, not just who he says he is or who you want him to be. Dating also helps *you* find out what you want—and what you *don't* want—when you are ready to make a commitment to someone. And even if your date doesn't end up being the love of your life, you might still be lucky enough to have found a new friend.

MY FIRST "OFFICIAL" DATE was with a guy I thought of as a friend. We were hanging-out buddies and always had fun together. But, with time, he became adamant about taking me out on a date to a swish local restaurant and treating me to a breaded veal cutlet, a dish I'd never tasted. (It was delicious.) After our dessert of pie à la mode, he told me how serious he felt about me and how he'd like us to go steady. I just couldn't do it. He was my pal, and I knew there was no way I could ever feel romantic about him. Unfortunately for me, after the cutlet, he could no longer see me as just a friend. As much as I missed being around him, I understood that our friendship had changed. But I've had a soft spot for breaded veal ever since.

Dating. What a concept. I wish I'd done more of it. I was always in a hurry to have a boyfriend or go steady. Sometimes I rushed into seeing someone exclusively before I really knew who he was and gave him qualities that he didn't even possess.

Probably **MY WORST DATE** (and, trust me, everyone is bound to have some clunkers) was with a fellow who picked me up with his driver, barely looked at me, and spoke about nothing but his elderly mother and his prize St. Charles spaniel. (He even carried a picture of the pooch, impeccably groomed atop a plush velvet doggy bed. Sheesh!) Not only was this guy a drip, he was obviously already seriously attached and unavailable.

Saving the very best for last, **MY MOST MEMORABLE DATE** was with a man I met through a friend at an impromptu dinner party. I had arrived late, and when our eyes met we both smiled. He took me out for lunch a few days later, and we enjoyed each other's stories and company. He was European and smelled divine. The next day I received this telegram (left) from him.

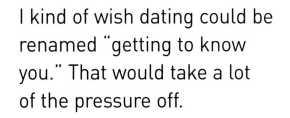

FAXGRAM®

99 WEST SHEFFIELD AVENUE ■ ENGLEWOOD, NEW JERSEY 07631

```
TNCH
C037 252-1 L995 68 09/04/81 03:40 LS
6A 09/04 03:37 I045 46-1 C037 252 09/04/81 03:39
RGE046 VIA ITT GXI883  DP4131TG010
UINX CO DPFF 013
FRANKFURT AM MAIN/TF 13/12 04 0923


KIM CATTRAL
122 NORTH LUCERNE
LOS ANGELES, CA 90004


I LIKE THE WAY YOU  WALK

COL LOSANGELESCA(90004) 122
```

Western Union **Mailgram**
THIS MAILGRAM MESSAGE WAS TRANSMITTED ELECTRONICALLY

Admittedly, I'm not the expert on dating that, say, Samantha is but, looking back on those early dates (blind or otherwise), I'm embarrassed to tell you not only how nervous I was but also how much I cared. And of course you should care. But when I was younger I had a tendency to take it all too seriously.

I kind of wish dating could be renamed "getting to know you." That would take a lot of the pressure off.

BOYFRIEND Material

Having a boyfriend is great...*if* he's the right guy. Many girls will tell you they have a "type"—a look or a personality that they find appealing, even irresistible. You may like them tall and clean-cut, your best friend swoons over boys with long hair, the smarter the better for your cousin, and your neighbor goes for guys in trouble like a kitten for catnip. The type of person you're attracted to says something about you—what you value, what you aspire to, even what you're rebelling against.

Whether it's football padding, bling, or a spot on the math team that gets under your skin, be aware that in going for a certain type, you are projecting your own romantic fantasy onto that person. If you find that you're consistently attracted to guys who are unavailable, unattainable, or even worse, unkind to or bad for you, then you need to gain some control over your choices and understand why you make them. There is never a good excuse for anyone to harm you emotionally or physically, and you should never tolerate this behavior. The answer to why you would choose someone who abuses you lies within yourself.

If you think being with a guy will make you complete, solve all your problems, or make you more popular, then chances are you're not going to have a healthy relationship. He's not your answer— you are. It all goes back to self-esteem again.

If you value yourself, have a solid support group (girlfriends who love you and are honest with you), and can stand up for what you believe in, you'll have a much better chance of picking the right guy—and losing the wrong guy.

This guy's a keeper:

You can communicate honestly and openly with each other.

He thinks you're beautiful the way you are.

He doesn't insist on always seeing you away from your friends and family.

He makes an effort to explore the things you like and to get to know the people you love.

When you're around him, you feel like you can really be yourself.

He doesn't pressure you into doing things you don't want to do.

Reasons to throw him back:

- He's verbally or physically abusive.
- He never wants to do anything but have sexual contact or be alone together.
- He is addicted to drugs or alcohol and unwilling to get help.
- He cheats or lies.
- He tries to keep you all to himself and makes no effort to get to know your friends and family.
- He can't make you laugh.

Romeo *Wasn't* Built in a Day

Romance and fantasy will always be linked. Since we were little girls, we've dreamed of having someone to call our own. Our vision of who that person will be is one that we continually shape as we learn more about ourselves, the world, and the people and places that hold promise for making dreams come true.

The first stages of falling in love always involve being able to imagine ourselves with someone. Once involved, we daydream about that person for pleasure. For practicality, we make plans (another form of fantasy) that include them. This is totally natural, but frequently—*very* frequently—our fantasies just don't match who our boyfriends really are.

What sometimes happens next is that, rather than trying to revise the fantasies we've been nurturing in private for so long, we set about trying to revise our boyfriends. For some crazy reason, we think it's easier. It isn't. At this point, I would suggest it's time to reevaluate. And that means reevaluating everything: your dreams, your guy, your own inability to be flexible or tolerant. Something's gotta give, and experience has taught me that it isn't going to be the guy.

You might be able to refine him, re-dress him, loosen him up, or button him down, but you'll never really change him, nor should you. People only change from the inside out—and only when they themselves really want to.

Relationships are about mutual respect, acceptance, support, communication, thoughtfulness, tenderness, sharing, and enjoying each other's company.

The Lab Book
OF LOVE

You only met him three weeks ago, but neither of you can think or do anything that doesn't involve the other. You've never felt like this before. You want to write his name across the sky. Is it a crush, pure madness, or could it be...LOVE? Let's consult the book—the lab book, that is.

Science and romance are two words you don't typically hear in the same breath, but over the last several years, medical research has increasingly turned its attention to matters of the heart. The findings are fascinating and help to explain a lot.

Researchers took people who described themselves as "madly in love" and put them through a brain scanner while showing them pictures of their lovers. Lo and behold, they noticed that the part of the brain associated with basic drives like hunger and thirst and mechanisms that produce the kind of euphoria associated with addiction were all activated.

Apparently, when you're in love, your brain experiences an addictive response driven by a deep human survival need. No wonder you can't sleep or eat!

So that's why we love. Oh, and let's not forget summer nights, starry skies, and the moon up above.

When It's Over...

You put your heart and soul into this relationship, and now it's over. There will never be anyone else like him, and you're certain that you'll never love again. How could your life be over so soon? What's the point of even getting out of bed?

Whether you broke off with him or he broke off with you, give yourself some time to grieve. A big part of your life is gone.

You are allowed to cry.
You are allowed to write long letters to him—but never send them.
You are allowed to call your best friend and tell her your heart is breaking.

In fact, you *should* be doing all these things. Getting all the old stuff out of your system is a necessary part of making room for whatever's in the future (even if, right now, you don't feel like you have much of a future without him). Measure your success in relationships not by the number of boyfriends you've had, but by how well you take what you've learned from past relationships and apply it to your life.

My first serious boyfriend was tall, blond, and handsome. He had lived in the big city of Toronto before moving to my little hometown, so he had an air of sophistication as well. We met in high school, and before long we became serious. But there were conflicts. I had a crazy workload, studying and participating in local speech arts and drama festivals. This didn't leave me very much free time, and my lovely new beau just didn't react very well to that.

I felt I always had to choose between him and the rest of my life, which tormented me because I loved him deeply and didn't want to disappoint him. When I told him of my plans to attend acting school in New York, he just lost it. I actually became afraid to break up with him because of his possessiveness and bad temper.

I did go to New York, though, and after a few months of upsetting letters and phone calls, we finally stopped communicating. This was heartbreaking for me, and it took me almost a year to even think about dating again. In that year, I grew to understand that our relationship hadn't been healthy for either of us. We didn't want the same things. I wanted to explore the world and myself in it, and he wanted to explore having a family. When I finally got through the sadness, I felt a great sense of relief and freedom.

TORONTO, 19 YEARS OLD. GETTING OVER MY FIRST BIG LOVE.

Chapter Six

SEXUAL *Intelligence*

At the time in your life when you're thinking more about developing a loving relationship with a partner, you're probably also thinking about how far that relationship might go. In other words, you're thinking about SEX. Whether or not you want to have it. Whether or not it's right. Whether or not you're the only one *not* doing it. (I can guarantee you, you're not—despite the bragging you might hear in your school hallways.) And you *should* be asking yourself these questions. Sex can be a wonderful experience, but the consequences of becoming sexually active can be both good and bad.

Your first partner should be someone really special, someone you trust completely, someone you can always count on....

Your first partner should be *you*.

Sex is a natural and healthy part of your life. And exploring your own body will help you understand how it works and what it can do. It will also give you pleasure and the knowledge of what feels good, and what doesn't. But when it comes to myths about exploring your own sexuality, masturbation could win an award for most misunderstood form of self-gratification. It won't make you blind, cause you to break out, or spoil sex with a partner. And—surprise—girls do it, too.

IMAGINE THAT!

Imagination plays a *hugely* important role in human sexuality, and sexual fantasies are a big part of that. Having them doesn't mean you are weird, even if the fantasies seem really weird. Remember, fantasies are not meant to represent real life but, rather, the wild and wonderful landscape of your imagination. In the privacy of your own mind, you're free to realize the pleasure of sex without the realities, responsibilities, and restrictions that come along with sex in the real world.

I remember first exploring my sexuality after seeing an Elvis Presley movie. (Elvis of the 1960s.) I recall lying in bed and wrapping my arms lovingly around myself as I imagined sweet kisses from Elvis. Meantime, I was actually kissing my pillow. I was in heaven and felt a strong urge of desire.

I'm not sure if Elvis just seemed too real, but it wasn't long before I abandoned him for someone more fantastical—Count Dracula. The idea of someone superhuman made it easier for me to let go, I guess. Also, it was exotic and exciting.

At the time, I was confused and ashamed that this kind of "weird" fantasy would arouse me. I felt disconnected from it and never told anyone. I felt like Dracula was my "dirty secret." Now I realize just how natural these fantasies are. My image of Dracula stealing into my bedroom to take me while I slept allowed me to feel sexual pleasure—without guilt.

What Would SAMANTHA Do?

There was only one time on the set of *Sex and the City* that the scriptwriters and I disagreed about "what Samantha would do," and that came up in an episode about a young woman and sexual readiness.

In seven years of doing the show, I literally never questioned the storylines given to me. I recognized that they were provocative and risk-taking, but I always felt they came from a spirit I could get behind and, hopefully, make funny and real. Then one day, I was handed a scene involving Samantha, a thirteen-year-old girl, and oral sex. In the heat of the scene, Samantha becomes defensive and in retaliation brags about her knowledge of and technique for performing the sexual act.

This was something I just absolutely could not see Samantha doing. This was also personal; my niece was thirteen at the time, and the whole scenario offended me. That Samantha would act competitively with another person over a sexual technique was unflattering enough, but with a minor? The whole idea was just nuts.

I understood that some thirteen-year-old girls do engage in sexual activity, but I also felt there had to be a better comment we could make on the situation. After a few rounds of rewrites, we resolved the scene by having Samantha try to provide a life lesson, advising the girl that being sexually active represents a conscious decision to step forward into adulthood, with all of its responsibilities. She spoke not just about the risk of disease or pregnancy, but also about the responsibility girls have to their own growth and development.

We get to be girls just once—and women for a whole lot longer. Childhood is a lot to leave behind.

> Becoming sexually active is a conscious decision to step forward into adulthood, with all of its responsibilities.

Samantha Jones seems to know all about sex. And thanks to some great scriptwriters, she has an answer for every question. I, on the other hand, have come by my knowledge of sexuality the old-fashioned way: through life's experiences.

The ==RIGHT== Time

For some, the decision about when to have sex for the first time is a no-brainer because of deeply held beliefs about waiting for marriage. For others, the question of when, where, and how their virginity might end can seem like a minefield. Advising people you don't know on the matter definitely has its perils, and I hope you'll cut me some slack as I tiptoe through, delicately.

Only YOU will know when you're ready for sex.

So many girls struggle with the very important question of when they're ready for sex. My advice is this: If you're wrestling with the question, you're not ready. Take your time. When a girl asks "How can I possibly keep myself from having sex with my boyfriend?," it's time to engage in the full-frontal discussion.

Your feelings about sex and sexuality are influenced by the times in which you're growing up as well as by your parental upbringing. And it's different for every person.

When you're struggling with a decision this big, no pamphlet or Web site is a substitute for a good, old-fashioned heart-to-heart. If you feel comfortable sharing this question with someone you trust—an older sibling or cousin, a mentor, your mom— reach out. You may worry that discussing sex with someone you look up to will be awkward but, chances are, your confidante will be empathetic and will welcome the opportunity to give you sound advice and the benefit of her experience.

So while no one but you can say when you're ready for sex, here is a *partial* list of reasons why it might be better to wait.

It's *not* the right time for sex if:
- He'll leave you if you don't do it.
- You think it will prove to him that you really love him.
- All the other girls are doing it, and you think it's uncool not to.
- You don't know how to say no.
- You're doing it on a dare.

And don't even *think* about it unless:
- You have a strong bond of trust with your partner.
- You'd still be together even without sex.
- You and your partner have educated yourselves about—and obtained— birth control and protection from sexually transmitted infections.
- You are free to change your mind at any time.

Sex Doesn't Just HAPPEN

On TV and in the movies, sex just seems to happen. The music comes up, the lights go down, and suddenly everybody's naked. In real life, first sex that "just happens" could be the worst sex you'll ever have. You might fear that planning for sex— talking to your partner, visiting your doctor, and using a condom—takes away from the romance, but let me assure you, the opposite is actually true. It's dealing with an unexpected pregnancy, a sexually transmitted infection, or a one-night stand that will stop romance dead in its tracks. Prepare yourself for sex—*before* you get naked. I promise, the hearts and flowers will flow even more freely because you're looking after yourself.

A caring partner will be just as concerned as you are about things like sexually transmitted infections, unintended pregnancies, and broken hearts, but you should always make sure that *you* have all your bases covered. Don't leave it up to him.

Be Informed about STIs

Sexually transmitted infections (STIs), also known as sexually transmitted diseases (STDs), can be a serious consequence of unprotected sexual contact—whether it's vaginal, anal, or oral sex.

A few of the more common STIs include chlamydia, genital herpes, gonorrhea, HIV/AIDS, human papillomavirus (HPV), and syphilis.

Each condition can come with symptoms such as genital warts, bumps, blisters, itchiness, and soreness. Some symptoms are more severe than others—and sometimes, people who have been infected show no signs at all. So it's best to be informed. If you've had unprotected sex and you're worried, or if you just want to learn more, you can contact your local public health department or check their online resources. Your public and school libraries will also have information. Or talk to your doctor.

Here's how to reduce your risk of getting or spreading an STI:

- Abstinence (not having sex, including oral sex).
- Always use a condom. There is no better way to protect yourself.
- If you're sexually active, get tested for STIs regularly. And if you have had unprotected sex, see your doctor immediately.
- If you are diagnosed with an STI, follow through with your complete course of treatment as prescribed by your doctor.

When You *Don't* Want to Have Sex

You *always* have a choice about whether to have sex.

Just because you've said yes to a partner once—or many times—does not mean you have to have sex with him every time he wants to, or that you have to do it with anybody else who asks. You are not a slut or a tease if you change your mind about having sex. The decision is yours to make *every* time sex is in question. Anyone who tells you that you want to when you really don't is more interested in his needs than in your feelings. Is that really the kind of partner you're looking for?

When "No" Is Not Enough

I have never been the victim of a sex crime. That's not because I live in a safe neighborhood or because I am someone in the public eye. Rape can happen to anyone at any time. It is an act of violence. Men who commit rape are deeply screwed up. He could be the stranger you pass on the street or the guy who's just asked you out.

Living a life of fear is not the answer to protecting yourself, but being aware and prepared can save your life physically *and* emotionally. I believe that it's a good idea for women to be trained in some form of self-defense. If a situation arises where you need to protect yourself, you'll be that much more confident and ready. There are various hotlines you can call and Web sites you can visit that can give you information and/or support.

THE JOY OF **SAFE** SEX

Making the decision about if or when to have sex may not be easy.
But whenever you believe you are completely ready, sex can be a
fulfilling emotional and physical experience for you.

MY FIRST PROFESSIONAL
HEAD SHOT AS A CONTRACT
PLAYER AT UNIVERSAL STUDIOS.
I'M 20 YEARS OLD.

Chapter Seven

GIRL MEETS *World*

ARE WE THERE YET?

Growing up doesn't happen magically when you reach your goal of graduating from high school or college, starting your first job, or finding your mate. It happens by living and the choices you make. Someone once told me to imagine my life the way I'd like it to be and to live accordingly. That sounded like good advice—until a small complication called "reality" got between me and my credit card.

What I *have* found useful throughout my life is to remain curious about what I don't know, listen to my instincts, and use my own judgment to guide me. This takes what growing up takes: patience.

When I'm faced with an important decision, I've learned to STOP and think through my options before taking action—to consider how a decision will affect both me *and* the people around me, and to weigh the consequences before letting my emotions rule.

Growing up means taking responsibility for *you*. It doesn't mean you can't ask for counsel or help; it just means that you have to pilot your life while staying aware of what's going on around you and listening to your gut. One thing is for sure: you'll face the same challenges over and over until you've learned that lesson—and then, guess what? You're just in time to start on the next challenge.

YOU'RE GOING TO SPEND THE REST OF YOUR LIFE GROWING UP—AND SO IS EVERYBODY ELSE.

Other people are just working on different areas of growth than you are. No matter how old they are, how much money they have, or where they went to school. So relax. Oh, and before I forget... Growing up can be a lot of *fun*, too!

Your First Home *Away from Home*

A SUMMER SUBLET. SLEEPIN' ON THE COUCH.

There's nothing like having your own space, whether it's a shared college dorm, a sublet with four other girls, or your own studio-apartment oasis. It's all yours (and your roommates').

My first apartment was a summer sublet on Manhattan's Upper East Side. Jen and I slept on couches, while our lucky roommate got the private bedroom. (My negotiating skills have improved since then.) At the end of the summer, Jen and I got our own apartment, which we furnished in a style I like to call Starving Student Lite, with cots up against the brick wall and summer deck chairs given to us on loan. Depressing. "The bare essentials" was my home design for most of my late teens and early twenties—dingy, tiny spaces with little or no furniture. These were the days before IKEA, so inexpensive options were limited.

On the next page, I've listed a few essentials (besides a Roommate Cleanup-duty Chart) **that will help you make the most of what you can afford.**

Light

We all need it! Open your shades or curtains, and let the daylight stream in. It will brighten your spirits as well as the room. At night, candles, table lamps, or floor lamps give a warmer, cozier glow than harsh fluorescent light.

Entertainment

Whether you have a used mini system or an iPod, fill your life with special tunes. As for books and DVDs… Favorite ones are like old friends and should never be left behind, no matter where you move.

Flowers

There is no simpler way of bringing life into your living space than fresh-cut flowers or a flowering plant. Don't wait for someone else to buy them—buy them for yourself.

Decoration

Search art-gallery gift shops or poster shops for an artist's work that speaks to you. Or look for a poster of a favorite film or person that inspired you, made you laugh, or moved you. I have framed Matisse prints on my wall that I collected as a teenager, and they still give me great pleasure. I also cherish my niece's third-grade original masterpiece "Christmas with Dalmatian Dot."

Furniture

Check newspaper ads to find deals on furniture, or take advantage of friends moving out and blowout sales at big department stores. I stripped antiques and used brightly colored blankets to cover up crazy patterns on used couches and chairs. And I always made sure I had lots of large, decorative pillows that could be moved around the apartment for guests to get comfy on. They're a good, inexpensive substitute for furniture in a small space.

What nourishes *you* in your home?

Focus on what you can have in your life on a regular basis. Diamonds make me smile— but they come later and go on a different list.

121

Keeping Tabs

One of the biggest challenges of leaving home is managing your resources—not only your inner ones but your outer ones as well. In other words, money. There wasn't much to go around in my home, so I didn't have much experience in handling it when I left for New York. My first bank account was a revelation. I worked as a waitress between acting jobs and banked my entire paycheck while eating (mostly at the restaurant) and living on my tip money and income from babysitting. It was an exacting science not to dip into my earnings. I made a list of what my essential monthly costs were and never bought any extras until I had those costs covered. Fortunately, I didn't grow up in a world where teenagers had credit or debit cards, or else I would have been even more challenged to stay within my budget.

Here are some things that living within a budget has taught me:

- **Go for quality over quantity.** "A rich man pays once—the poor man, many times." I've learned that old adage the hard way, when I've been suckered by cheaper brands that looked good but didn't last very long or wear as well as something that would have cost a little more. Now, when I buy, I get the best quality I can afford.

- **Shop at reputable stores and check the return and refund policies before you buy.** It seems obvious, but doing this has saved me a lot of time and money. I've even learned to keep the receipt!

- **Try not to impulse-shop.** When shopping for a big purchase, if you're not in love with your choice, put it on hold and come back the next day with a refreshed eye and one of your girlfriends.

ESSENTIAL Pieces

Auditions are an important part of working as an actor, and it definitely pays to be prepared. When I was pounding the pavement, I made sure my wardrobe complimented the roles I was being considered for.

Whether you're applying for a job or a scholarship, meeting your boyfriend's parents, or raising funds for a worthy cause, you should present yourself as the confident, polished person you are. The visual is key to people's first impression of you.

When you start a professional wardrobe on a budget, find your main pieces first. For the four main characters on *Sex and the City*, Pat Field, our costume designer, chose wardrobe staples based on each character's career needs.

As a young professional, you'll find that a few classic pieces are worth a lot more to you than a closet full of trendy special-occasion clothes. For example, I started with two well-tailored suits within my budget: one that came with a skirt, the other with pants. Then I added a couple of bright silk blouses. I also found a simple black cocktail dress, and a shawl wrap for all occasions.

That Little Black Dress you've heard about is a must-have.

The rest is all about the accessories, and you can really have fun with those. It's worth investing in a pair of classic black pumps, a pair of strappy two-tone heels, a good-sized purse with clean lines, and a small black evening purse. Fake diamond studs are always a good choice for eveningwear jewelry, and fabulous silver or gold hoops are great for daytime, along with any fun costume jewelry ring that takes your fancy. These were my staples, and I added to them a little at a time. And don't forget—sales, sales, sales!

THE LITTLE BLACK DRESS.
STILL A WARDROBE STAPLE, WHETHER YOU DRESS IT UP OR DOWN.

Acting the Part

Getting a job, living well on your own, and handling your own finances properly are certainly things that show the world you are becoming a responsible, independent person. *Acting* like one is one more thing that shows you're moving smoothly into the world. When you meet new people at this stage in your life, their first impressions of you have less to do with your family (whom they don't know), your history, or your past accomplishments (neither of which they know about unless you tell them) than with how you present yourself here and now.

Be present when you meet someone—don't be half there—and when you're with people, *listen* to them. Think about how pleased you are when someone you've met only once and haven't seen in a while remembers not only your name but also the details of what you discussed when you met. It makes you feel like the other person considers you important.

Being able to cultivate that feeling in others is an invaluable skill when you are starting your new and independent life, making new friends, and establishing professional relationships.

BOOKSIGNING AT HARRODS, LONDON, 2005.

> "I have a daily religion that works for me. Love yourself first and everything else falls into place. You really have to love yourself to get anything done in this world."
>
> —Lucille Ball

Being *You*

NEW YORK CITY, 2005.

Trust one of my favorite comediennes to sum up the main message I hope you've picked up from the pages of this book: that everything *really does* begin and end with YOU when it comes to your life.

Your family, friends and experiences may help shape your character. But, ultimately, *you* are responsible for finding your own way to true adulthood—with all its challenges and rewards. And the journey starts by acknowledging, loving and respecting who *you* uniquely are, BEFORE you start striving for what you want or who you'd like to be in the world.

I've shared with you some of the events and experiences that have influenced and inspired me over the years. I hope they've been of some use. I didn't grow up by myself—I had a lot of help—and it didn't happen overnight. I've had tremendous support and guidance over the years, and continue to receive that from the people close to me. I feel very lucky that I've survived the odds and still love what I chose to do with my life.

Yeah, I have regrets that I didn't have time to do it ALL, but that's part of growing up too—accepting what is, and enjoying what you *did* get to have and accomplish.

It's a terrific ride—especially when you keep your eyes open.

Much love and support.

ACKNOWLEDGMENTS

The idea for *Being a Girl* was fueled by the young women who have reached out over the years. Your questions and concerns inspired and shaped this book. It is dedicated to you.

A huge transatlantic hug goes to London cartoonist Martha Richler, aka Marf, whose miraculous riot of original art rolling off our printers never failed to inspire us—brilliantly capturing the text in its own enchanting way. To designer Gorette Costa, we owe a huge debt for her remarkable instincts, creativity, and supergirl endurance in bringing the book to life. And special thanks to editor Mireille Majoor, whose solid groundwork helped us at every step.

Love and thanks to Jennifer Gelfer, for her honesty in sharing a difficult life lesson with us and for her invaluable input and council over the years and through so many creative projects. We thank the beautiful Kyra Panchenko for all her "beauty secrets" as well as her nurturing care on and off set.

Thank you to the Cattrall family for more than could be said with words, but also for painstakingly rummaging through boxes of memorabilia, making this project possible.

Giant thanks to all at Madison Press who have nurtured and protected *Being a Girl* from its inception. The encouragement, friendship, and guidance of Wanda Nowakowska, Brain Soye, and Oliver Salzmann go beyond measure. Thank you as well to the sharp-eyed Imoinda Romain for keeping us moving from outline to layouts.

As always, thank you to Larry Kirshbaum and Maureen Regan—our storybook godparents in publishing. And to Cindy Eagan at Little, Brown Books for Young Readers, as well as all the international publishers who have supported this book with such enthusiasm. Finally, thank you to the amazing Amanda Enright for keeping the engines stoked and the home fires burning at Fertile Ground Productions.

—Kim Cattrall and Amy Briamonte

SELECTED BIBLIOGRAPHY

Anderson, Walter. *The Confidence Course*. New York: HarperPerennial, 1998.

Branden, Nathaniel. *Honoring the Self*. New York: Bantam, 1985.

Brumberg, Joan Jacobs. *The Body Project*. New York: Random House, 1997.

Carlson, Richard, Ph.D. *Don't Sweat the Small Stuff for Teens*. New York: Hyperion, 2000.

Daldry, Jeremy. *The Teenage Guy's Survival Guide*. New York: Little, Brown and Company, 1999.

De Botton, Alain. *How Proust Can Change Your Life*. New York: Vintage, 1997.

Drill, Esther, and Heather McDonald, and Rebecca Odes. *The Looks Book*. New York: Penguin, 2002.

Strauch, Barbara. *The Primal Teen*. New York: Anchor Books, 2004.

Wiseman, Rosalind. *Queen Bees and Wannabes*. California: Three Rivers Press, 2003

Editorial Director
WANDA NOWAKOWSKA

Editorial Assistance
IMOINDA ROMAIN

Book Design
COSTA LECLERC DESIGN INC.

Production Manager
SANDRA L. HALL

Publisher
OLIVER SALZMANN

Vice President, Business Affairs and Production
SUSAN BARRABLE

Printed by
IMAGO PRODUCTIONS (F.E.) LTD., SINGAPORE

being a girl

was produced by
MADISON PRESS BOOKS